Taking Off
Beginning English

Second Edition

Susan Hancock Fesler
Christy M. Newman

McGraw-Hill

Taking Off Beginning English, 2nd Edition

Published by McGraw-Hill ESL/ELT, a business unit of The McGraw-Hill Companies, Inc. 1221 Avenue of the Americas, New York, NY 10020. Copyright © 2008 by The McGraw-Hill Companies, Inc. All rights reserved. No part of this publication may be reproduced or distributed in any form or by any means, or stored in a database or retrieval system, without the prior written consent of The McGraw-Hill Companies, Inc., including, but not limited to, in any network or other electronic storage or transmission, or broadcast for distance learning.

ISBN 10: 0-07-338458-5 (Student Book)
ISBN 13: 978-0-07-338458-0 (Student Book)
    5 6 7 8 9 DOW/DOW 11 10

ISBN 10: 0-07-719304-0 (Student Book with Audio Highlights)
ISBN 13: 978-0-07-719304-1 (Student Book with Audio Highlights)
  2 3 4 5 6 7 8 9 DOW/DOW 11 10 09 08

Project manager: Linda O'Roke
Cover designer: Wanda Espana
Interior designer: Aptara
Artists: Anna Divito, Nancy Carpenter, Roberta Rieple, Mick Reid

McGraw-Hill

www.esl-elt.mcgraw-hill.com

Cover image: Anna Divito

Acknowledgments

The authors and publisher would like to thank the following individuals who reviewed the *Taking Off* program at various stages of development and whose comments, reviews, and assistance were instrumental in helping us shape the project:

Janelle Baker
HARRIS COUNTY DEPARTMENT OF EDUCATION
HOUSTON, TX

Donna Champion
SONOMA COUNTY LIBRARY
ADULT LITERACY PROGRAM
SANTA ROSA, CA

Carole Chinn-Morales
CITY COLLEGE OF SAN FRANCISCO
SAN FRANCISCO, CA

Leslie Clark
CITY COLLEGE OF SAN FRANCISCO
SAN FRANCISCO, CA

Natacha Cruz
MIAMI SENIOR ADULT SCHOOL
MIAMI, FL

Ann Marie Damrau
SAN DIEGO COMMUNITY COLLEGE DISTRICT
SAN DIEGO, CA

Sally Gearhart
SANTA ROSA JUNIOR COLLEGE
SANTA ROSA, CA

Maura Gisbert
MIAMI SENIOR ADULT SCHOOL
MIAMI, FL

Maria Elena Gonzalez
ADULT LITERACY RESOURCE INSTITUTE
UNIVERSITY OF MASSACHUSETTS, BOSTON
BOSTON, MA

Susan Gordon
CITY COLLEGE OF SAN FRANCISCO
SAN FRANCISCO, CA

Mary Kapp
CITY COLLEGE OF SAN FRANCISCO
SAN FRANCISCO, CA

Millard Lightburn
MIAMI SENIOR ADULT SCHOOL
MIAMI, FL

Arturo Maldonado
MIAMI SENIOR ADULT SCHOOL
MIAMI, FL

LaRanda Marr
OFFICE OF ADULT EDUCATION
OAKLAND UNIFIED SCHOOL DISTRICT
OAKLAND, CA

Anne Molina
EVANS COMMUNITY ADULT SCHOOL
LOS ANGELES UNIFIED SCHOOL DISTRICT
LOS ANGELES, CA

Patricia Mooney-Gonzalez
NEW YORK STATE DEPARTMENT OF EDUCATION
ALBANY, NY

Paula Orias
PIPER COMMUNITY SCHOOL
BROWARD COUNTY PUBLIC SCHOOLS
SUNRISE, FL

Sylvia Ramirez
COMMUNITY LEARNING CENTER
MIRACOSTA COLLEGE
OCEANSIDE, CA

Mercy Rivas
MIAMI SENIOR ADULT SCHOOL
MIAMI, FL

Susana Rodas
MIAMI SENIOR ADULT SCHOOL
MIAMI, FL

Mary Ann Siegel
ALBANY PARK COMMUNITY CENTER
CHICAGO, IL

Lynda Terrill
CENTER FOR APPLIED LINGUISTICS
WASHINGTON, D.C.

Dave VanLew
SIMI VALLEY ADULT & CAREER INSTITUTE
SIMI VALLEY, CA

To the Teacher

Taking Off Second Edition is a four-skills, standards-based program for beginning students of English. Picture dictionary art pages teach life-skills vocabulary in a clear and visual way. The gradually accelerating pace of the book instills confidence in students as they establish a solid foundation in the basics of English.

Taking Off Second Edition Features

- **NEW** *Grammar* lessons summarize and provide practice on central grammar points in each unit.

- **NEW** *Read* lessons reuse and recycle vocabulary and grammar in new contexts as students practice finding the main idea and other comprehension skills.

- **NEW** *Write* lessons provide structured writing experiences that encourage students to personalize the vocabulary and grammar they have learned in the unit.

- **NEW** *My Life* activity boxes offer students the opportunity to personalize new vocabulary and concepts while participating in communicative activities.

- **NEW** *Our Cultures* sections with photos and graphic organizers help student discuss and compare their native cultures with their new culture.

- **Four-skills foundation course** prepares students for Book 1 in a variety of popular series, such as *All Star* and *Excellent English*.

- **Activities correlated to CASAS, EFF, LAUSD Course Outlines, and Florida Adult ESOL Syllabi** prepare students to master a broad range of critical competencies.

- **Picture dictionary art pages** highlight life-skills vocabulary in engaging contexts.

- **Listening activities** help students develop speaking, reading, and writing skills in a low-anxiety environment.

- *Numbers* **pages** in each unit help students build numeracy skills for basic math work.

- *Community* **pages** in each unit introduce students to critical civics topics.

Components

- **Student Book** has twelve 16-page units with a wealth of individual, pair-, and group-work activities. In four special sections throughout the book, students and teachers will also find new *Review* lessons for additional study and practice. Listening scripts are found at the back of the Student Book and in the Teacher's Edition.

- **Student Book with Audio Highlights** provides students with audio recordings of all the vocabulary in the Student Book. This CD also includes recordings of all the *Read* lessons in the units.

- **Workbook** includes supplementary practice activities correlated to the Student Book. A flexible set of activities correlated to each unit builds vocabulary, listening, reading, writing, and test-taking skills. As a bonus feature, the Workbook also includes online activities for students to do in a computer lab or at home.

- **Literacy Workbook with Audio CD** incorporates phonics activities, letter and number practice activities, and "on-ramp" activities for emerging literacy students. This component is designed for students who do not have foundational literacy skills in their first language. The Literacy Workbook offers supplementary activities for each unit in the Student Book.

- **Teacher's Edition with Tests** provides:
  - Step-by-step teaching instructions
  - Over 300 expansion activities including Literacy Development activities and Extra Challenge activities
  - 50 reproducible worksheets, many of which offer creative tasks tied to the "big picture" unit openers
  - Culture, Literacy, and Pronunciation Notes
  - Two-page test for each unit
  - Audio scripts for audio program
  - Answer keys for Student Book, Workbook, and test materials.

- **Post-Testing Study Guide** provides reproducible worksheets to help students create performance portfolios that document post-testing readiness.

- **NEW** **Character Cards** stimulate conversation in the classroom with lively visual and conversation cues for the teacher to use. Durable, full-color cards provide ideal teacher presentation tools.

- **Color Overhead Transparencies** encourage teachers to present new vocabulary and concepts in fun and meaningful ways. This component provides a full-color overhead transparency for each of the "big picture" unit openers.

- **Audio Program** contains recordings for all listening activities in the Student Book. Listening passages for each unit test are provided at the end of the audio section for that unit.

Program Overview

Consult *Welcome to Taking Off* on pages xviii-xxiii. This guide offers teachers and program directors a visual tour of one Student Book unit.

Predictable lesson format

Student Book lessons are one page in length and contain three to five activities. This one-page format allows teachers to "chunk" their instruction into short, manageable sessions that give students a sense of accomplishment in their swift completion of each lesson. The first activity usually asks students to listen to and repeat new vocabulary and language. These listen and repeat activities help students prepare for speaking, reading, and writing skills in a low-anxiety environment. At the low beginning level, it is critical that students have a chance to listen to and repeat all new vocabulary and language before being asked to speak, read, or write.

Unit-opening illustrations

Each unit opens with a dynamic, full-page color illustration, providing context for the key vocabulary items and language presented in the unit. This illustration sets the scene for the unit, activating students' background knowledge and encouraging them to share words they can say in English. Teachers can present the unit-opening illustrations on an overhead projector with the Color Transparencies.

CASAS, EFF, LAUSD Course Outlines, and Florida Adult ESOL Syllabi

Program directors and teachers are often asked to benchmark student progress against national, state, or district standards. With this in mind, *Taking Off* carefully integrates instructional elements from a wide range of standards. Here is a brief overview of our approach to meeting these standards:

- **CASAS** Many states in the U.S. tie funding for adult education programs to student performances on the Comprehensive Adult Student Assessment System (CASAS). The CASAS (www.casas.org) competencies identify more than 300 essential skills that adults need in order to succeed in the classroom, workplace, and community. Examples of these skills include: identifying or using appropriate non-verbal behavior in a variety of settings, responding appropriately to common personal information questions, and comparing price or quality to determine the best buys. *Taking Off* carefully integrates CASAS competencies that are appropriate for low beginning students.

- **EFF** Equipped for the Future (EFF) is a set of standards for adult literacy and lifelong learning, developed by the National Institute for Literacy (www.nifl.gov). The organizing principle of EFF is that adults assume responsibilities in three major areas of life—as parents, citizens, and workers. These three areas of focus are called "role maps" in the EFF documentation. In the parent role map, for example, EFF addresses these and other responsibilities: participating in children's formal education and forming and maintaining supportive family relationships. Each *Taking Off* unit addresses one or more of the EFF role maps. The focus on the student as community citizen is particularly strong in Lesson 9 of each unit, which is devoted to *Community* activities.

- **LAUSD Course Outlines** were developed to guide teachers in lesson planning and to inform students about what they will be able to do after successful completion of their course. The LAUSD course outlines focus on acquiring skills in listening, speaking, reading, and writing in the context of everyday life. *Taking Off* addresses all four language skills in the contexts of home, community, and work, with appropriately targeted vocabulary for Beginning Low adult ESL students.

- **Florida Adult ESOL Syllabi** provide the curriculum frameworks for all six levels of instruction; Foundations, Low Beginning, High Beginning, Low Intermediate, High Intermediate, and Advanced. The syllabi were developed by the State of Florida as a guide to include the following areas of adult literacy standards: workplace, communication (listen, speak, read, and write), technology, interpersonal communication, health and nutrition, government and community resources, consumer education, family and parenting, concepts of time and money, safety and security, and language development (grammar and pronunciation). Each *Taking Off* unit carefully integrates these standards.

Number of hours of instruction

The *Taking Off* program has been designed to accommodate the needs of adult classes with 70–216 hours of classroom instruction. Here are three recommended ways in which various components in the *Taking Off* program can be combined to meet student and teacher needs.

- **70–120 hours** Teachers are encouraged to work through all of the Student Book materials, incorporating the *Review* and *Our Cultures* lessons as time permits. The Color Transparencies and Character Cards can be used to introduce and/or review materials in each unit. Teachers should also look to the Teacher's Edition for teaching suggestions and testing materials as necessary. *Time per unit: 7–10 hours.*

- **120–168 hours** In addition to working through all of the Student Book materials, teachers are encouraged to incorporate the Workbook and/or Literacy Workbook for supplementary practice. *Time per unit: 10–14 hours.*

- **168–216 hours** Teachers and students working in an intensive instructional setting can take advantage of the wealth of expansion activities threaded through the Teacher's Edition to supplement their use of the Student Book and Workbook materials. *Time per unit: 14–18 hours.*

Assessment

Some teachers prefer to evaluate their students informally by monitoring their students' listening and speaking abilities during pair-work or group-work activities. These teachers may also maintain portfolios of student writing to show the progress students are making in writing skill development.

For teachers who need or want formal assessments of their students, the Teacher's Edition provides two-page, reproducible tests for each Student Book unit. Each test takes approximately 30 minutes to administer, and these tests are designed to assess vocabulary, grammar, writing, listening, and reading comprehension skills, as well as grammar and writing development. There is a listening activity on each test, and the recorded passages for these sections are found on the Student Book Audio Program. Audio scripts for the tests appear in the Teacher's Edition.

SPECIAL FEATURES

Grammar Pages

Fundamental grammar points, such as nouns, pronouns, and adjectives, basic past and present tenses, and simple question forms are newly incorporated into each unit. These two-page descriptive *Grammar* spreads provide summary charts or visual explanation of important grammar points covered in each unit followed by activities that progress from highly to less structured.

Read and *Write* Pages

Simple but exciting readings about the lives and adventures of characters in *Taking Off* can be found in Lesson 12 of each unit. These readings use the vocabulary of the unit to expand reading and comprehension skills, including the critical skill of understanding the main idea. The complexity of the readings develops from basic realia-based readings to three-paragraph challenging, engaging stories. Each reading rests on a foundation of state and national standards, such as positive parental involvement or understanding bank forms.

Lesson 13, the *Write* page, provides a model of an important, standards-based writing skill, such as completing a form, writing a letter to the landlord requesting a repair, or preparing a health plan. Following the model, students are given the opportunity to complete a form with personalized information. These activities progress from highly structured to more and more independent writing choices as students move through the units.

Numbers pages

Learning basic math skills is critically important for success in school, on the job, and at home. Accordingly, most national and state-level standards for adult education mandate instruction in basic math skills. With this in mind, Lesson 8 in each Student Book unit is dedicated to helping students develop numeracy skills they need for basic math work. In Unit 1, for example, students learn the numerals 1–10 and the English words for these numbers. Labeled *Numbers*, these lessons enable students to complete activities on working with American money, reading temperatures, and understanding numbers on a paycheck.

Community pages

Many institutions focus direct attention on the importance of civics instruction for English language learners. This type of instruction is often referred to as *EL/Civics* and is designed to help students become active and informed community members. Lesson 9 in each Student Book unit explores a community- or work-related topic. Labeled *Community*, these lessons have areas of focus like learning about reading safety signs, writing a check, using an ATM, learning about health insurance, having a potluck dinner, and going to garage sales.

Classes with literacy and low beginning students

A special *Taking Off Literacy Workbook* has been designed for literacy students enrolled in low beginning classes. Most low beginning students are true beginners in English who are literate in their first language. Literacy students, on the other hand, usually do not have fundamental first-language literacy skills. Literacy students often need specific instruction in letter formation, phonics, and other fundamental reading, listening, and writing skills.

As teachers who have worked with mixed groups of literacy and low beginning students know, dealing simultaneously with the needs of each of these groups of learners is a great challenge. The Literacy Workbook offers a unique resource for teachers in such multi-level classes. Each Literacy Workbook unit provides essential support for key elements of the Student Book. Working with or without a teacher's aide, literacy students can tackle basic reading, listening, and writing activities in the Literacy Workbook while their low beginning classmates tackle tasks at their ability level.

The *Taking Off* Cast of Characters

Taking Off features an engaging cast of characters enrolled in a beginning English class. The authors developed the book around these characters to help students learn new language from familiar faces.

Carlos Avila
Waiter, *Brazilian*

Maria Cruz
Salesclerk, *Mexican*

Leo Danov
Taxi driver, *Russian*

Sandy Johnson
Teacher, *American*

Tien Lam
Delivery person, *Vietnamese*

Ben Lee
Construction worker, *Chinese*

Grace Lee
Homemaker, *Chinese*

Paul Lemat
Computer programmer, *Haitian*

Isabel Lopez
Office worker, *Colombian*

Nadira Shaheed
Health aide, *Somali*

Scope and Sequence

Unit	Topics	Listening & Speaking Skills	Reading & Writing Skills	Grammar
1 **Welcome to the classroom.** *Page 2*	• Meeting new people • The alphabet • Greetings • Countries • Classroom language • Classroom objects • Emergency form • Homework • Learning log	• Introduce yourself • Say the name of the country you come from • Listen and identify classroom objects • Say your telephone number, address, and email address • Ask for and give the spelling of words • Listen to and practice simple dialogs • Follow classroom directions	• Read & write alphabet letters • Interpret basic sight words • Write proper names, countries, and classroom words • Examine classroom commands/directions • Write and read personal information • Check new vocabulary in a learning log	• *I'm, It's* • *What's*
2 **Where are you from?** *Page 18*	• Native language • Country of origin • Marital status • Physical appearance • Address • U.S. map • Identification form	• Collect information from classmates • Ask and answer about country of origin • Ask and answer about the language you speak • Recognize differences in marital status • Discuss height and color of eyes and hair	• Fill in information on a chart • Write personal information statements • Use writing to describe height • Identify vocabulary that describes physical appearance • Read and write words for select countries and languages • Read a map of the USA • Write about your teacher • Write about new students	• *Am, Is, Are* • *Has/Have*
3 **This is my family.** *Page 34*	• Relatives • Name titles *(Mr., Mrs., Ms., and Miss)* • Family tree • Ages • Family form • Children	• Ask questions about family • Discuss family members with classmates • Ask about someone's age • Listen to information about family members • Say name titles *(Mr., Mrs., Ms., Miss)* • Recognize numbers 20-100	• Write family position words to complete a sentence • Read names using titles *(Mr., Mrs., Ms., Miss)* • Make your own family tree • Read a paragraph about a family member • Identify the topic of a story • Complete a family form	• *Yes, I do. / No, I don't.* • *My, His, Her, Your, Their*

Review for Units 1–3 *Page 50*
• Matching Activity: personal information
• Listening Activity: marital status
• Grammar: present tense of *Be* and *Have*

Our Cultures: Greetings *Page 52*
• Identify different types of greetings
• Complete a Venn Diagram to compare greetings in different countries
• Discuss forms of greetings in groups

Numeracy	Community Awareness	Florida Standards	CASAS	EFF	LAUSD Beginning Low
• Learn numbers 1–10 • Identify numbers used in context • Say and write telephone numbers with area code • Say and write addresses and email addresses	• Complete an emergency form • Identify your emergency contact person • Learn 911 for police and fire emergencies	**1:** 1.05.01 **2:** 1.17.02 **3:** 1.17.02 **4:** 1.15.02 1.15.03 **6:** 1.09.03 **7:** 1.09.03 **8:** 1.09.03 **9:** 1.09.03 **12:** 1.16.11 **13:** 1.15.05	**1:** 0.1.1, 0.1.4 **4:** 0.1.6 **6:** 0.1.5 **8:** 0.1.1 **9:** 0.1.1, 0.1.5 **10:** 6.0.1 **13:** 0.2.1 **13:** 0.2.2 **13:** 2.1.2	• Speak So Others Can Understand • Listen Actively • Cooperate With Others • Take Responsibility for Learning	LIFE SKILLS • 1 • 5 • 9a, b • 18 • 16 • 17 • 15 • 58a GRAMMAR • 13a • 16c (i)
• Learn numbers 11–19 • Say and write numbers in an address • Say and write zip codes	• Complete a detailed identification form • Learn to write your name as follows: last name, first name, middle initial • Learn the components of an address	**1:** 1.05.02 **2:** 1.05.02 **3:** 1.05.02 **6:** 1.15.06 **8:** 1.15.05 **9:** 1.15.05 **10:** 1.16.02 **11:** 1.16.02 **12:** 1.13.03 1.13.04	**1:** 2.7.2 **2, 3:** 0.1.3 **4:** 0.1.2 **5:** 1.1.4, 1.1.9 **6:** 0.2.1 **8:** 2.4.1, 6.0.1 **9:** 0.2.2 **12:** 2.2.5	• Read with understanding • Convey Ideas in Writing • Cooperate With Others • Reflect and Evaluate	LIFE SKILLS • 2 • 4 • 5 • 6 • 7 • 23b GRAMMAR • 1 • 20
• Learn numbers 20-100 • Say your age • Recognize number words • Write the ages of family members • Write the number of people in your family	• Complete a form about your family • Politely decline to answer a question	**1:** 1.14.01 **2:** 1.14.01 **3:** 1.14.01 **4:** 1.14.01 **8:** 1.08.01 **9:** 1.08.01 1.14.01 **11:** 1.16.10 **13:** 1.15.06	**1:** 7.5.5 **2, 3:** 7.4.8 **6:** 2.7.3 **7:** 0.1.6 **8:** 6.0.2 **9:** 5.3.1, 0.2.2 **12, 13:** 0.2.3	• Convey Ideas in Writing • Resolve Conflict and Negotiate • Use Math to Solve Problems and Communicate • Learn Through Research	LIFE SKILLS • 4 • 6 • 7 • 9c • 60 • 10c • 17 GRAMMAR • 16a, b

Scope and Sequence

Unit	Topics	Listening & Speaking Skills	Reading & Writing Skills	Grammar
4 **Welcome to our house.** *Page 54*	• Rooms in a house • Items in a house • Types of houses • Household needs • Your dream house • Garage sales	• Listen to and recognize the rooms in a house • Discuss household items • Learn the names of different types of housing • Speak with a partner about household items and needs • Differentiate between numbers that sound alike (18 vs. 80).	• Write the names of the rooms in a house • Review a paragraph about a new apartment • Write and read about a dream house • Read a paragraph about garage sales • Write a note about a household problem	• Singular and Plural Nouns • *a* and *an*
5 **I talk on the phone.** *Page 70*	• Daily activities • Days of the week • Months and dates • Time • Appointments • Medical form • Birthdays	• Discuss your daily activities • Listen to and say the days of the week • Listen to and say the months of the year • Listen to and say times • Talk about birthdays • Use the telephone to make appointments • Listen to ordinal numbers	• Read the time on analog and digital clocks • Recognize abbreviations for months • Write times on a calendar • Write and read ordinal numbers • Read about a birthday • Write about what you see in a picture • Write an email	• Simple Present Tense
6 **Let's go shopping.** *Page 86*	• Clothes • Colors • Clothing sizes • Problems with clothing • Money • Paying by check	• Listen to and identify articles of clothing • Ask for what you need in a store • Ask about clothing size • Say that clothing is too large or small • Say color words • Ask about favorite colors • Play a spoken guessing game with classmates	• Read and write clothing words • Write sentences about clothing size • Write about problems with clothes • Learn words for American coins and bills • Write a check • Read a catalog • Write a shopping list • Write about favorite clothes	• Adjectives and Nouns

Review for Units 4–6 *Page 102*
• Matching activity: answers to *Wh-* questions
• Reading activity: interpret an internet page
• Grammar: singular/plural nouns, simple present tense

Our Cultures: Homes *Page 104*
• Identify types of houses from different cultures
• Compare your house to your house in your native country
• Discuss types of housing in groups

Numeracy	Community Awareness	Florida Standards	CASAS	EFF	LAUSD Beginning Low
• Differentiate between numbers with similar digits • Complete sentences using numbers • Associate numbers above one with plural forms	• Learn that garage sales are community activities • Recognize the different types of houses in a community • Ask a landlord for household repairs	**4:** 1.11.06 **11:** 1.16.06 **12:** 1.11.06	**1:** 1.4.2 **2, 3:** 7.4.3 **4:** 1.4.1 **7:** 7.1.1 **8:** 6.0.1 **9:** 8.3.2 **13:** 1.4.7	• Advocate and Influence • Solve Problems and Make Decisions • Plan • Use Information and Communications Technology	LIFE SKILLS • 4 • 14a • 38 • 39 • 60 GRAMMAR • 9a, b
• Practice ordinal numbers • Recognize the days and dates on a calendar • Write your date of birth on a form • Write month, date, and year in numerical form (MM/DD/YY)	• Complete a medical form • Learn about the following services: dental cleaning, car tune-up, and haircut • Keep community appointments on a calendar	**2:** 1.08.03 **3:** 1.08.03 **4:** 1.08.02 **5:** 1.08.02 **6:** 1.06.01 **8:** 1.08.04 **9:** 1.15.05 **10:** 1.16.02 **11:** 1.16.02	**1:** 0.2.4 **2, 3:** 2.3.2 **4, 5:** 2.3.1 **6:** 2.1.8, 7.1.4 **7:** 7.1.2 **8:** 0.2.1, 6.0.1 6.0.2 **9:** 3.2.1 **12:** 2.7.1 **13:** 4.6.2	• Listen Actively • Solve Problems and Make Decisions • Plan • Use Math to Solve Problems and Communicate	LIFE SKILLS • 3 • 12 • 25 • 26 • 27 • 60 GRAMMAR • 1a, b
• Write a check • Recognize American coin and bill denominations • Match coins and bills to monetary values • Recognize page references	• Ask for assistance in a store • Buy clothes in a store • Buy clothes from a catalog • Recognize and use American money	**3:** 1.15.01 **4:** 1.15.01 **5:** 1.15.01 **6:** 1.11.02 1.11.04 **7:** 1.11.02 1.11.04 **8:** 1.11.03 **9:** 1.08.07 1.11.01 **10:** 1.16.06 1.16.07 **11:** 1.16.06 1.16.07 **R:** 1.11.02	**1:** 0.1.3, 1.3.9 **2:** 1.3.3 **3:** 0.2.4, 8.1.2 **4:** 1.2.5 **5:** 1.3.4, 7.5.1 **6:** 1.1.9, 1.2.1 **7:** 1.2.1, 1.2.2 **8:** 1.1.6, 1.2.2 6.0.2 **9:** 1.2.4, 1.8.2 **12:** 1.3.4 **13:** 1.2.1	• Read with understanding • Observe Critically • Advocate and Influence • Use Math to Solve Problems and Communicate	LIFE SKILLS • 11b • 14a • 30a, b • 31 • 32 • 33 • 34 • 60 GRAMMAR • 12a, b

Scope and Sequence

Unit	Topics	Listening & Speaking Skills	Reading & Writing Skills	Grammar
7 **I'm so hungry!** *Page 106*	• Grocery shopping • Food • Food groups • Containers for food • Meals • Supermarket coupons • Potluck dinner	• Listen for the names of food items • Talk about what food items you need • Discuss breakfast, lunch, and dinner foods • Order in a restaurant • Ask and answer questions about foods you eat • Discuss frequency of activities	• Make a shopping list • Read the names of food items • Complete a chart about location of foods in a supermarket • Read a paragraph about potluck dinners • Read supermarket coupons • Identify true and false statements about a reading	• Count Nouns • Non-count Nouns
8 **How's the weather?** *Page 122*	• Weather • Seasons • Leisure activities • Temperature (Fahrenheit and Celsius) • U.S. map • Weather Map	• Discuss different types of weather • Listen to and discuss leisure activities • Discuss activities you like to do in different seasons • Listen to a weather report • Talk about temperature in a city	• Read and write about the seasons • Recognize weather-related vocabulary • Write sentences about weather • Interpret a weather map • Make a chart about weather in your country • Read an email • Write a letter to a friend	• Present Continuous Tense • Contractions
9 **Where's the post office?** *Page 138*	• Neighborhood map • Places in the community/ neighborhood • Banking • ATM (Automated Teller Machine)	• Talk about places you see in your neighborhood • Ask and answer questions about the location of neighborhood places • Ask your classmates what places they live near • Ask your classmates where they do things	• Read a neighborhood map • Write sentences about the location of neighborhood places • Read about depositing money into a savings account • Read about how to use an ATM • Read about cashing a check • Complete a supermarket card club application	• Prepositions of place

Review for Units 7–9 *Page 154*
• Group discussion: "What are you doing now"?
• Writing activity: containers
• Listening activity: identify words in a short dialog
• Grammar: contractions with *be,* present continuous tense

Our Cultures: Marketplaces *Page 156*
• Talk about marketplaces in other countries
• Complete a chart on food shopping
• Discuss food shopping in groups

Numeracy	Community Awareness	Florida Standards	CASAS	EFF	LAUSD Beginning Low
• Write times of the day for meals • Use times of the day in sentences • Use container words to talk about food (a bunch of grapes) • Identify what you can afford with an amount of money	• Explore a supermarket • Learn about a potluck dinner • Practice ordering food in a restaurant • Use supermarket coupons • Make a shopping budget	**1:** 1.07.06 **2:** 1.07.06 **3:** 1.07.06 **4:** 1.07.07 **5:** 1.07.07 **6:** 1.07.08 **8:** 1.11.02 **10:** 1.16.06 **11:** 1.16.06 **12:** 1.08.05 **R:** 1.07.06	**1:** 1.3.8 **2:** 1.3.8 **3:** 0.1.2, 1.3.7 **4:** 3.5.2, 8.2.1 **5:** 8.2.1 **6:** 2.6.4, 8.1.3 **7:** 3.5.9, 8.2.1 **8:** 1.1.4, 1.1.7 **9:** 2.7.2, 2.7.3 **12:** 1.2.3, 1.3.5 **13:** 1.3.4 **14:** 0.1.3 **R:** 7.4.3, 7.4.7	• Speak So Others Can Understand • Guide Others • Take Responsibility for Learning • Reflect and Evaluate	LIFE SKILLS • 12 • 13 • 14a • 31 • 32 • 35 • 36 • 37 GRAMMAR • 9d
• Interpret a thermometer in degrees Fahrenheit and Celsius • Write numbers using degrees Fahrenheit and Celsius	• Read a weather map • Practice personal correspondence • Talk about the weather in your community • Discuss community related leisure activities	**1:** 1.13.01 **2:** 1.13.01 **3:** 1.13.01 **6:** 1.13.01 **7:** 1.13.01 **9:** 1.13.01	**1:** 2.3.3, 5.7.3 **2:** 1.1.5, 2.3.3 **3:** 5.7.3 **4:** 0.2.4 **5:** 0.1.6 **6:** 0.2.4, 7.5.6 **7:** 2.63, 2.3.3 **8:** 1.1.5, 6.6.4 **9:** 1.1.3, 2.3.3, 6.6.5 **12:** 4.6.2 **13:** 7.4.2 **R:** 7.4.2, 7.4.8	• Convey Ideas in Writing • Observe Critically • Learn Through Research • Use Information and Communications Technology	LIFE SKILLS • 14a • 13 • 28 • 29 • 60 GRAMMAR • 2 • 3
• Read dates and money amounts on a bank deposit slip • Find information on a deposit slip • Complete a bank withdrawal • Use an ATM PIN number • Read about subtraction of a fee from a check	• Interpret a neighborhood map • Recognize business in your community • Practice banking procedures • Understand check cashing fees • Fill out an application form	**1:** 1.12.02 **2:** 1.09.02 1.09.03 **3:** 1.12.02 **4:** 1.08.06 **7:** 1.12.02 **8:** 1.08.06 **10:** 1.16.08 **11:** 1. **12:** 1.08.07 **13:** 1.08.07	**1:** 5.6.2 **2:** 2.2.1, 2.2.5 **3:** 2.5.4, 2.6.1 **4, 5:** 2.2.1 **6:** 0.1.6 **7:** 0.2.4, 2.4.2 **8:** 1.8.2 **9:** 1.8.1 **12:** 1.8.2 **13:** 0.2.2	• Read with understanding • Listen Actively • Guide Others • Use Information and Communications Technology	LIFE SKILLS • 7 • 11a, b • 13 • 22 • 23a, b • 30a, b GRAMMAR • 14a, b • 14c, d

Scope and Sequence

Unit	Topics	Listening & Speaking Skills	Reading & Writing Skills	Grammar
10 **You need to see a doctor.** *Page 158*	• Health problems • Body parts • Medicine • Healthy food • Exercise • Health insurance	• Discuss health problems and remedies • Listen and identify health information in dialogs • Express physical pain • Make a doctor's appointment for your relative • Discuss medicines e • Listen to information about health insurance	• Recognize words for physical ailments • Read about staying fit and healthy • Write a phone conversation • Read a health insurance card • Fill in an insurance information form • Complete a Venn diagram to compare healthy habits • Write a health plan	• Action Verbs • Negatives
11 **What's your job?** *Page 174*	• Jobs • Workplaces • Driving • Want ads • Safety signs • Paychecks • Job applications • Job items • Work Skills	• Talk about jobs • Say what job conditions you like (indoors, with people) • Say what work-related skills you can do (fix things) • Ask and answer questions with affirmative and negative responses • Ask classmates about their past occupations	• Examine the tools different jobs require • Complete sentences about what you and others can do • Read want ads • Read safety signs • Fill in a form about what your job was before • Complete sentences about paychecks • Read and fill out a job application	• Simple Past of *Be* • *Can / Can't*
12 **How do you get to school?** *Page 190*	• Transportation • Directions to places in the community • Public transportation • Learner's permit • Road signs • Bus schedule	• Practice dialogs about methods of transportation • Differentiate among left, right, and straight ahead • Follow directions in the community • Listen to dialogs about time phrases • Ask about train and bus schedules	• Use a community map to give directions • Analyze a bus schedule • Complete sentences about a learner's permit • Read and respond to road signs • Read a story and answer question about driving with a new baby • Read and write about how to get to school	• Questions with *Be* • Questions with *Do / Does*

Review for Units 10–12 *Page 206*
• Group discussion about personal skills
• Matching activity: questions and answers
• Listening activity: identify health problems and times in dialogs
• Grammar: simple past tense of *Be, Can / Can't*

Our Cultures: Transportation *Page 208*
• Identify forms of transportation in other countries
• Complete a chart comparing transportation and lifestyle
• Discuss transportation in groups

Numeracy	Community Awareness	Florida Standards	CASAS	EFF	LAUSD Beginning Low

• Learn about health insurance co-payments
• Say medicine dosages and frequency words
	• Complete health insurance forms
	• Understand a doctor's role in the community
	• Read medicine labes from a community pharmacy
	• Learn about healthy habits
	• Make a plan to stay healthy
		1: 1.07.01
		   1.07.02
		2: 1.07.01
		   1.07.02
		4: 1.07.03
		6: 1.07.07
		8: 1.07.04
		9: 1.01.06
		10: 1.16.02
		11: 1.16.02
		13: 1.07.04
			1, 2: 3.1.1
			3: 3.1.2, 3.1.3
			4: 3.3.1
			5: 3.4.3
			6: 3.4.5, 3.5.9, 7.5.4
			7: 3.3.3, 3.5.9
			8: 3.3.2
			9: 3.2.3
			12: 3.5.2
			13: 3.5.2
			R: 8.3.1
				• Observe Critically
				• Guide Others
				• Advocate and Influence
				• Solve Problems and Make Decisions
					LIFE SKILLS
					• 7
					• 19
					• 43
					• 44
					• 45
					• 46
					• 60
					
					GRAMMAR
					• 5
					• 19

• Understand paycheck deductions
• Learn about hourly wages
• Review concept of depositing money in bank account
	• Examine various jobs in the community
	• Recognize want ads as a community resource
	• Learn about safety signs
	• Gain information about the job application process
	• Complete an application form
		1: 1.01.01
		   1.03.02
		2: 1.01.01
		   1.03.02
		3: 1.01.01
		   1.03.02
		5: 1.01.04
		6: 1.01.07
		   1.02.01
		7: 1.01.04
		8: 1.02.05
		9: 1.02.03
		10: 1.16.02
		12: 1.01.03
		13: 1.06.02
		   1.06.03
			1: 4.1.6, 4.1.8
			2: 4.1.6, 4.1.8
			3: 4.1.9
			4: 4.4.2
			5: 4.4.2
			6: 4.1.3
			7: 4.1.2, 4.4.7
			8: 4.2.1
			9: 4.3.1
			12: 4.1.1
			13: 4.4.3
			R: 4.1.3
				• Speak So Others Can Understand
				• Cooperate With Others
				• Resolve Conflict and Negotiate
				• Reflect and Evaluate
					LIFE SKILLS
					• 19
					• 48, 49
					• 50, 51
					• 52, 53
					• 54, 55
					• 56a, b
					
					GRAMMAR
					• 4a, b, c
					• 6
					• 7

• Read times related to public transportation
• Practice time phrases
	• Read schedule for community transportation
	• Review various forms of transportation (bus, train, subway)
	• Read about car safety equipment
	• Get around your community
		1: 1.09.01
		2: 1.09.03
		3: 1.09.03
		4: 1.09.03
		6: 1.09.02
		   1.09.04
		7: 1.09.02
		   1.09.04
		9: 1.08.02
		10: 1.16.02
		11: 1.16.02
		12: 1.14.05
		R: 1.09.01
		   1.09.02
			1: 2.2.3
			2, 3: 1.9.4,
			   2.2.1,
			   2.2.5
			4: 0.1.2, 2.2.2
			5: 2.2.4
			6: 1.9.2, 2.5.7
			7: 1.9.1, 2.2.2
			8: 2.2.4, 4.2.1,
			   6.6.6
			9: 2.2.4, 4.2.1
			12: 3.5.7,
			   3.5.9
			13: 2.2.5
				• Resolve Conflict and Negotiate
				• Solve Problems and Make Decisions
				• Take Responsibility for Learning
				• Learn Through Research
					LIFE SKILLS
					• 7, 13
					• 11a, b, c
					• 14a, b
					• 23a, b
					• 24a, b
					• 42, 60
					
					GRAMMAR
					• 17

Welcome to *Taking Off*

- **"Big picture" unit openers** highlight life-skills vocabulary in engaging contexts.

- **Recurring cast of characters** helps student learn new language from familiar faces.

- **"Big picture" scenes** are springboards to a wealth of all-skills expansion activities in the Teacher's Edition.

- **Color Transparencies** for the "big picture" openers provide fun and meaningful ways to present new vocabulary and concepts.

- **Predictable unit structure** includes the same logical sequence of 16 lessons in each unit.

- **Listening preparation activities** help students develop speaking, reading, and writing skills in a low-anxiety environment.

- **Guided speaking tasks** encourage students to immediately practice new language with a partner.

- **Standards-based lesson content** prepares students to develop key CASAS, EFF, LAUSD Course Outlines, and Florida Adult ESOL Syllabi competencies.

- **Audio support** is available on the Student Book audio program. Additional listening activities are recorded on the Literacy Workbook audio CD.

- *My Life* communicative tasks personalize new vocabulary and concepts.

- *Numbers* **page in each unit** helps students build numeracy skills for basic math work.

- **Life-skill contexts** provide real-life applications for numeracy work.

- **Helpful reminder notes** offer tips for successfully using new language.

- **Communicative activities** allow students to practice everyday conversations with their classmates, using the vocabulary and grammar they have learned.

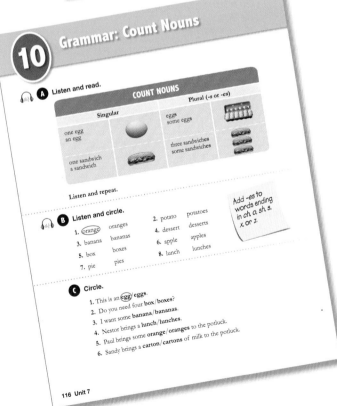

- *Community* page in each unit focuses on developing students' roles in life as workers, parents, and citizens.

- **Real-life documents and situations** expose students to critical concepts they encounter at work, at home, and in the community.

- **Real-life document practice** gives students the chance to fill out documents they often encounter outside the classroom.

- **Clear and concise grammar charts** introduce grammar points in easily comprehensible chunks.

- **Margin boxes** remind student of relevant information that was introduced earlier in the text.

- **Tightly controlled activities** allow student to focus on the structure of the new grammar point.

- **Realia-based readings** like maps, advertisements, coupons, descriptive paragraphs, and catalog pages provide the basis for developing reading skills.

- **Reading activities** develop critical thinking skills by asking students to find important information and make inferences.

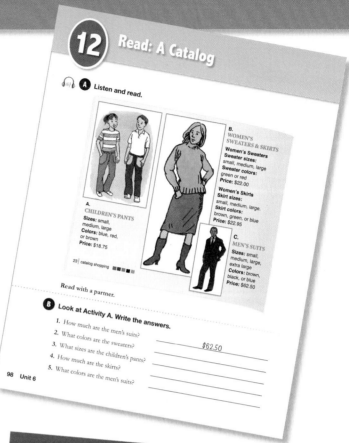

- *What do you know?* **lessons** at the end of each unit help students review, consolidate, and synthesize what they've learned.

- **Listening reviews** help teachers assess listening comprehension, while giving students practice with item types and answer sheets they encounter on standardized tests.

- **Learning Logs** ask students to catalog the vocabulary, grammar, and life skills they have learned and determine what areas they need to review.

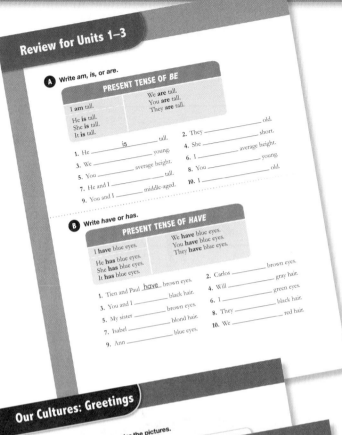

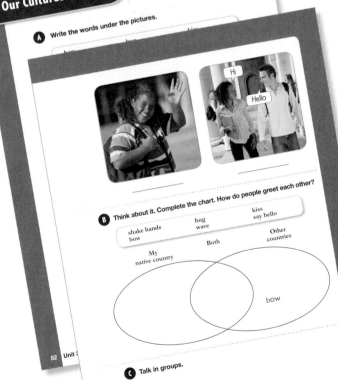

- **Review units** review fundamental grammar points such as the simple present of *be* and *have*.

- **Additional grammar practice** is also available in the *Taking Off Workbook*.

- ***Our Cultures*** pages use photo-based lessons to promote cross-cultural comparisons on topics such as greetings, marketplaces, transportation, and homes.

- **Graphic organizers** help students visually organize the key points of each *Our Cultures* lesson.

- **Communicative activities** provide informal speaking opportunities where students can compare and contrast their lives in their native cultures and in the United States.

Taking Off Ancillaries

Taking Off Teacher's Edition

NEW 300 expansion activities

NEW 48 reproducible worksheets

NEW Culture, Grammar, Pronunciation Notes

Taking Off Workbook

NEW Grammar activities

NEW Reading and Writing activities

NEW *Go online!* activities

Taking Off Literacy Workbook

NEW Phonics Section

NEW CDs included in every workbook

NEW Grammar, Reading, and Writing activities

Taking Off Transparencies Packet

Color Overhead Transparencies of "Big Picture" Unit Openers

NEW *Taking Off* Character Cards

Welcome to the classroom.

What's your name?

a b c d e f g

h i j k l m n o p

q r s t u v w

x y z

Sandy

Tien

Leo

Nadira

Ben

Grace

Maria

BINGO

Carlos

Paul

Isabel

Where are the students?
What do you see?

1 Welcome!

 A **Listen.**

Paul: Hello, I'm **Paul**.
Isabel: Hi, **Paul**. I'm **Isabel**. Nice to meet you.
Paul: Nice to meet you too, **Isabel**.

Listen and repeat.

B **Talk with a partner.**

A: Hello. I'm _____.
B: Hi, _____. I'm _____. Nice to meet you.
A: Nice to meet you too, _____.

 C **Listen.**

Carlos: Hi. I'm **Carlos**. I'm from **Brazil**.
Tien: Hello. My name is **Tien**.
I'm from **Vietnam**.

Listen and repeat.

D **Talk with 5 classmates.**

A: Hi, I'm _____. I'm from _____.
B: Hello. My name is _____. I'm from _____.

E **Read and write.**

Welcome to the classroom. 3

2 The Alphabet: A–M

A **Listen.**

| Aa | Bb | Cc | Dd | Ee | Ff | Gg | Hh | Ii | Jj | Kk | Ll | Mm |

Listen and repeat.

B **Say and write.**

| A | B | C | D | E | F | G | H | I | J | K | L | M |
| A | | | | | | | | | | | | |

| a | b | c | d | e | f | g | h | i | j | k | l | m |
| a | | | | | | | | | | | | |

C **Match.**

1.
A   d
B   c
C   a
D   e
E   b

2.
F   h
G   i
H   g
I   f

3.
J   k
K   m
L   j
M   l

D **Listen and write.**

1. a ___ ___
2. ___ ___ ___
3. ___ ___ ___
4. ___ ___ ___
5. ___

3 The Alphabet: N–Z

A Listen.

| Nn | Oo | Pp | Qq | Rr | Ss | Tt | Uu | Vv | Ww | Xx | Yy | Zz |

Listen and repeat.

B Say and write.

N	O	P	Q	R	S	T	U	V	W	X	Y	Z
___	___	___	___	___	___	___	___	___	___	___	___	___

n	o	p	q	r	s	t	u	v	w	x	y	z
___	___	___	___	___	___	___	___	___	___	___	___	___

C Listen and say the letters.

1. U S A
2. C H I N A
3. H A I T I
4. R U S S I A
5. B R A Z I L
6. M E X I C O
7. C O L O M B I A
8. S O M A L I A
9. V I E T N A M

D Listen and write.

1. __h__ __i__

2. ___ ___ ___

3. ___ ___ ___ ___

4. ___ ___ ___ ___

5. ___ ___ ___ ___ ___

6. ___ ___ ___ ___ ___

4 How do you spell that?

 A **Listen.**

Maria:	I'm **Maria Cruz**. What's your name?
Tien:	My name is **Tien Lam**.
Maria:	How do you spell that?
Tien:	My first name is **T-I-E-N**.
	My last name is **L-A-M**.

Listen and repeat.

B **Talk with 5 classmates.**

A: I'm _____. What's your name?
B: My name is _____.
A: How do you spell that?
B: My first name is _____.
My last name is _____.

MY LIFE **Write your name.**

First name: _____

Last name: _____

Circle the letters in your first name.

A B C D E F G H I J K L M
N O P Q R S T U V W X Y Z

Circle the letters in your last name.

A B C D E F G H I J K L M
N O P Q R S T U V W X Y Z

5 What's in the classroom?

 A Listen.

1. student

2. paper

3. desk

4. chair

5. pen

6. board

7. backpack

8. computer

9. teacher

10. notebook

11. door

12. book

Listen and repeat.

 B Listen.

Sandy: What's this?
Grace: A **backpack**.

Listen and repeat.

C Talk with a classmate.

A: What's this?
B: A _____.

6 Follow directions.

A Listen and read.

Circle.		book	(pen)
Check.		___ book	✔ pen
Complete.		It's a __book__.	
Fill in.		(A) pen	(B) book
Match.	b book	a.	
	a pen	b.	

B Circle.

Paul	paper	(pen)

backpack	board	computer

board	notebook	chair

C ✔ Check.

✔ student	___ book	___ desk

___ door	___ board	___ teacher

___ computer	___ door	___ board

7 Practice directions.

A Complete.

first	last	~~meet~~	name

1. Hello. Nice to _____meet_____ you.

2. I'm Maria Cruz. What's your _____?

3. My _____ name is Paul.

4. My _____ name is Lemat.

B Fill in.

    (A) paper   (B) notebook   (C) book

    (A) chair   (B) Carlos   (C) computer

    (A) Ben   (B) pen   (C) paper

C Match.

1. _b_ door

2. ____ notebook

3. ____ teacher

a.

b.

c.

Welcome to the classroom. 9

Open the book.

  A Listen.

1. open

2. close

3. take out

4. put away

5. go to

6. point to

Listen and repeat.

  B Listen and circle.

1.

2.

3.

4.

9 Point to the book.

🎧 **A** **Listen and fill in.**

1. Ⓐ Close the door.   Ⓑ Open the door.
2. Ⓐ Go to the board.   Ⓑ Point to the board.
3. Ⓐ Take out the pen.   Ⓑ Put away the pen.
4. Ⓐ Put away the notebook.   Ⓑ Point to the notebook.
5. Ⓐ Close the door.   Ⓑ Open the door.
6. Ⓐ Take out the paper.   Ⓑ Put away the paper.
7. Ⓐ Point to the desk.   Ⓑ Go to the desk.
8. Ⓐ Open the book.   Ⓑ Take out the book.

B **Write.**

1. Open the _____door_____.   2. Go to the _____.

3. Take out the _____.   4. Put away the _____.

5. Close the _____.   6. Point to the _____.

MY LIFE **Write directions.**

1. Go to the board _____.

2. _____.

3. _____.

4. _____.

5. _____.

Read your directions to your group.

My phone number is (981) 555-2305.

 A **Listen.**

0	1	2	3	4	5	6	7	8	9	10
zero	one	two	three	four	five	six	seven	eight	nine	ten

Listen and repeat.

B **Write the number.**

1. __6__ six   2. ____ four   3. ____ seven   4. ____ three

5. ____ zero   6. ____ ten   7. ____ two   8. ____ nine

9. ____ five   10. ____ one   11. ____ eight

 C **Listen.**

Carlos: My phone number is **(981) 555-2305**.

Leo: My address is **7 Paper Street**.

Grace: My email address is **glee93@takingoff.edu**.

For: 2305

Say: two-three-oh-five

Listen and repeat.

D **Write about you. Tell 5 classmates.**

My phone number is _____.

My address is _____.

My email address is _____.

 E **Listen and circle.**

1. (six)   seven   2. four   five

3. 2   10   4. 5 Pen Avenue   8 Pen Avenue

5. 555-8080   555-5050   6. (781) 555-6789   (781) 555-9876

11 Nestor's Homework

 A Listen and read.

Homework

This is Nestor's homework. It's in his backpack.
Nestor writes his name. He writes the alphabet.
He writes five numbers. His homework is complete.
Maria reads Nestor's homework.

Nestor Cruz

Homework

Write the alphabet. a b c d e f g h i j k l m n o p q r s t u v w x y z

Write five numbers. 1 2 3 4 5

Read with a partner.

B Look at Activity A. ✔ Check what you see.

I see...	Yes	No
alphabet	✔	
backpack		
book		
computer		
desk		
homework		
9 numbers		
paper		

Welcome to the classroom. 13

 A **Listen and circle.**

1. (What's)   What is   2. What's   What is

3. I'm   I am   4. I'm   I am

5. I'm   I am   6. I'm   I am

7. It's   It is   8. It's   It is

I am = I'm

It is = It's

What is = What's

B **Circle.**

1. **What's /I'm** Carlos.   2. **What's / I am** from Mexico.

3. **What is / It is** your name? 4. **It is / What is** Maria.

5. **I am / What's** this?   6. **It's / I'm** a backpack.

C **Write.**

1. I'm _____.

2. It's _____.

3. What's _____?

13 Read and Write: An Emergency Form

A Read.

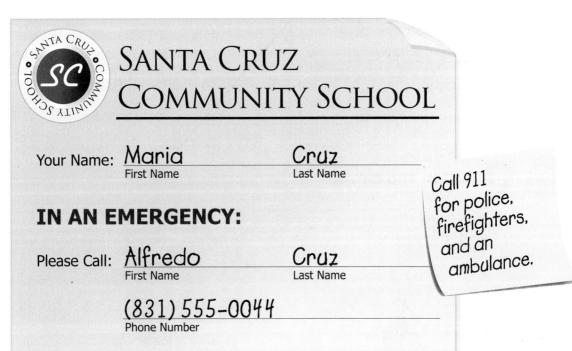

SANTA CRUZ COMMUNITY SCHOOL

Your Name: **Maria**   **Cruz**
First Name   Last Name

IN AN EMERGENCY:

Please Call: **Alfredo**   **Cruz**
First Name   Last Name

(831) 555-0044
Phone Number

Call 911 for police, firefighters, and an ambulance.

B Complete.

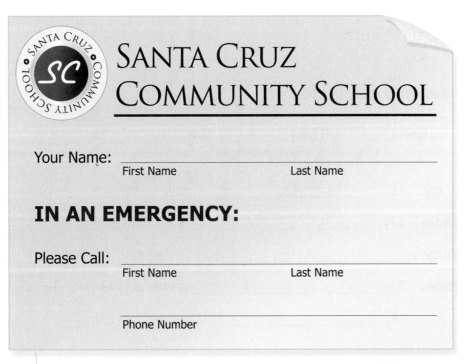

SANTA CRUZ COMMUNITY SCHOOL

Your Name: _____
First Name   Last Name

IN AN EMERGENCY:

Please Call: _____
First Name   Last Name

_____
Phone Number

What do you know?

 A **Listen and write.**

Sandy: Hello. I'm Sandy. What's your name?

Ben: My _____ is Ben.

Sandy: _____ to meet you, Ben.

Ben: Nice to _____ you too, Sandy.

 B **Listen and circle.**

1.

2.

3. Leo   Lopez

4. I-S-A-B-E-L   S-A-N-D-Y

5. (310) 555-0123   2039 Board Street

 C **Listen and complete.**

first	How	~~I'm~~	last	name

Sandy: Hi. _____I'm_____ Sandy. What's your name?

Grace: My _____ is Grace Lee.

Sandy: _____ do you spell that?

Grace: My _____ name is G-R-A-C-E.

My _____ name is L-E-E.

D Listen and write.

1. n __a__ m __e__

2. c l ___ ___ e

3. ___ o a ___ ___

4. b ___ ___ k

5. ___ e ___

6. s ___ ___ e ___

E ✔ Check the words you know.

Learning Log

✔ address	___ five	___ pen
___ alphabet	___ four	___ phone number
___ backpack	___ go to	___ point to
___ board	___ homework	___ put away
___ book	___ I am (I'm)	___ read
___ chair	___ It is (It's)	___ seven
___ check	___ last	___ six
___ circle	___ match	___ spell
___ classroom	___ meet	___ student
___ close	___ name	___ take out
___ complete	___ nice	___ teacher
___ computer	___ nine	___ ten
___ desk	___ notebook	___ three
___ door	___ numbers	___ two
___ eight	___ one	___ What is (What's)
___ email address	___ open	___ write
___ fill in	___ paper	___ zero
___ first		

LOOKING BACK Who do you see on page 2? Tell a partner.

Unit 2
Where are you from?

Where are the students?
What do you see?

1 Where are you from?

A **Listen.**

Leo: I'm from **Russia**. Where are you from?
Ben: I'm from **China**.

Listen and repeat.

B **Talk with a partner.**

A: I'm from _____. Where are you from?

B: I'm from _____.

C **Listen.**

Grace: Where is **Carlos** from?
Maria: **He's** from **Brazil**.
Grace: Where is **Isabel** from?
Maria: **She's** from Colombia.

Listen and repeat.

D **Talk with a partner.**

A: Where is _____ from?
B: He's | from _____.
    She's |

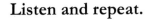

Word List

Grace/China
Leo/Russia
Carlos/Brazil
Maria/Mexico

2 What do you speak?

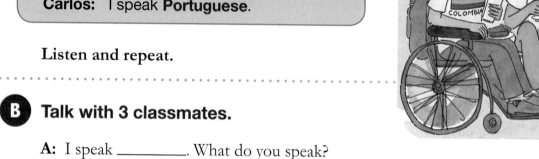

A Listen.

Isabel: I speak **Spanish**.
What do you speak?

Carlos: I speak **Portuguese**.

Listen and repeat.

B Talk with 3 classmates.

A: I speak _____. What do you speak?
B: I speak _____.

C Write about you.

My name is _____.

I'm from _____. I speak _____.

D Talk with 7 classmates. Complete the chart.

What's your name?	Where are you from?	What do you speak?
Nadira	Somalia	Somali

3   What does he speak?

  A   **Listen and read.**

Carlos   Tien   Ben   Maria

Name	Country	Speaks
Carlos	Brazil	Portuguese
Tien	Vietnam	Vietnamese
Ben	China	Chinese
Maria	Mexico	Spanish

B   **Listen.**

Paul: **Carlos** is from **Brazil**. What does **he** speak?

Grace: **He** speaks **Portuguese**.

Paul: **Tien** is from **Vietnam**. What does **she** speak?

Grace: **She** speaks **Vietnamese**.

Listen and repeat.

C   **Look at Activity A. Talk about Carlos, Tien, Ben, and Maria.**

A: _____ is from _____. What does _____ speak?
     (Name)   (Country)   (he/she)

B: _____ speaks _____.
     (He/She)   (Language)

Grace is married.

 A **Listen.**

1. married   **2.** single   **3.** divorced   **4.** widowed

Listen and repeat.

B **Listen and circle.**

 1.

2.

3.

4.

5 I am average height.

A **Listen.**

Paul: I am **average height.**
Leo is **tall.**
Tien is **short.**

Tien: Paul and Carlos are **average height.**

Listen and repeat.

Leo   Paul   Carlos   Tien

B **Talk with a partner.**

A: Tien and Maria are _____.
B: Grace is _____.
A: Sandy is _____ _____.

Tien   Maria   Sandy   Grace

C **Write about classmates.**

1. _____ Leo _____ is _____ tall _____.

2. _____ is _____.

3. _____ is _____.

4. _____ is _____.

5. _____ and _____

   are _____.

Read in groups.

6   We have brown eyes.

A **Listen.**

Leo has **green** eyes.
Isabel has **blue** eyes.
Carlos and Tien have **brown** eyes.
Tien has **glasses**.

Listen and repeat.

B **Talk about your classmates.**

_____ has _____ eyes. _____ and _____ have glasses.
  (Name)   (color)   (Name)   (Name)

C **Listen.**

Sandy: I have **red** hair.
         Ben and **Tien** have **brown** hair.
         Leo has **gray** hair.
         Isabel has **blond** hair.

Listen and repeat.

D **Write.**

1. I have _____ hair.

2. _____ has _____ hair.
    (Name)

3. _____ and _____ have _____ hair.
    (Name)   (Name)

7 He has brown hair.

A Write.

| blue eyes | gray hair | glasses | married |

1. _____gray hair_____

2. _____

3. _____

4. _____

 B Listen. Write the number.

____ Nadira

____ Sandy

____ Leo

_1_ Carlos

MY LIFE Bring a picture of a friend.
Talk in groups.

What's your address?

 A Listen.

11	12	13	14	15	16	17	18	19
eleven	twelve	thirteen	fourteen	fifteen	sixteen	seventeen	eighteen	nineteen

Listen and repeat.

B Write the numbers.

<u>11</u> ___ ___ 14 ___ 16 ___ ___ 19

C Write the numbers.

1. <u>11</u> eleven   2. ___ seventeen   3. ___ twelve   4. ___ fifteen

5. ___ sixteen   6. ___ thirteen   7. ___ eighteen   8. ___ fourteen

 D Listen.

Maria: What's your address?
Paul: My address is **1714 Brown Street**.
Maria: What's your zip code?
Paul: My zip code is **01313**.

Listen and repeat.

E Write about you.

My name is _____.

My address is _____.

My zip code is _____.

Read in groups.

9 An Identification Form

Community

A Read.

IDENTIFICATION FORM

TYPE OR PRINT

Danov   Leo   V
LAST NAME   FIRST NAME   MI

17 White Street   Los Angeles   CA   90011
ADDRESS   CITY   STATE   ZIP

CIRCLE ONE:

MARITAL STATUS: SINGLE   MARRIED   (DIVORCED)   WIDOWED

EYE COLOR: BLUE   BROWN   (GREEN)   BLACK

HAIR COLOR: BROWN   BLACK   (GRAY)   RED   BLOND

> MI = Middle Initial

B Complete.

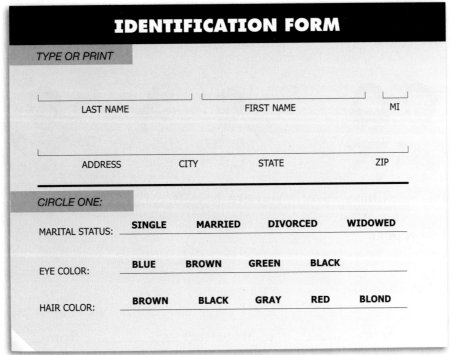

IDENTIFICATION FORM

TYPE OR PRINT

LAST NAME   FIRST NAME   MI

ADDRESS   CITY   STATE   ZIP

CIRCLE ONE:

MARITAL STATUS: SINGLE   MARRIED   DIVORCED   WIDOWED

EYE COLOR: BLUE   BROWN   GREEN   BLACK

HAIR COLOR: BROWN   BLACK   GRAY   RED   BLOND

Grammar: *Am, Is, Are*

 A Listen and read.

I am from Somalia.

We are from China.

Am, Is, Are		
I	**am**	from Somalia.
He	**is**	from Somalia.
She	**is**	from Somalia.
It	**is**	from Somalia.
We	**are**	from Somalia.
You	**are**	from Somalia.
They	**are**	from Somalia.

Listen and repeat.

 B Listen.

1.

I **am** from the USA.

2.

She **is** from Mexico.

3.

Carlos **is** from Brazil.

4.

We **are** from China.

5.

You **are** from Brazil.

6.

They **are** from China.

Listen and repeat.

C Write.

I _____ from _____. My teacher _____ from _____.

 28 Unit 2

Grammar: *Have/Has*

 A Listen and read.

Have/Has		
I	**have**	brown eyes.
He	**has**	brown eyes.
She	**has**	brown eyes.
It	**has**	brown eyes.
We	**have**	brown eyes.
You	**have**	brown eyes.
They	**have**	brown eyes.

Listen and repeat.

 B Listen.

1.

   I **have** blue eyes.

2.

   They **have** brown eyes.

3.

   You **have** brown hair.

4.

   Tien **has** glasses.

5.

   We **have** black hair.

6.

   He **has** green eyes.

Listen and repeat.

C Write.

I _____ _____ _____.

The teacher _____ _____ _____.

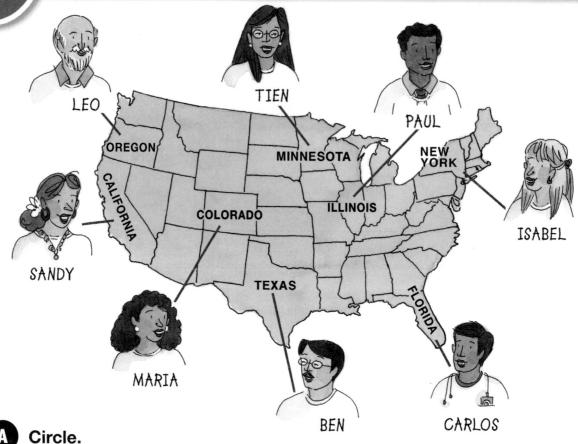

A Circle.

1. Sandy is in **Florida** / (**California**) / **New York**.

2. Tien is in **Texas** / **Minnesota** / **Oregon**.

3. Carlos is in **California** / **Florida** / **Texas**.

4. Isabel is in **California** / **New York** / **Colorado**.

5. Leo is in **California** / **Colorado** / **Oregon**.

6. Ben is in **Minnesota** / **Florida** / **Texas**.

7. Paul is in **New York** / **Florida** / **Illinois**.

8. Maria is in **New York** / **California** / **Colorado**.

B Write about you.

I'm in _____.

A **Write is, are, has, or have.**

Welcome New Students

Two new students _____ are _____

in Sandy Johnson's class. Nadira Shaheed

_____ from Somalia. Tien

Lam _____ from Vietnam.

Nadira _____ average height.

Tien _____ short. They

both _____ brown eyes.

Tien _____ glasses. Tien

_____ brown hair, but Nadira

_____ black hair. Both students

_____ happy in their new class!

Read with a partner.

B **Write about your teacher.**

    My teacher's name is _____.

My teacher is from _____.

My teacher is _____

and has _____ eyes and

_____ hair. My teacher

speaks _____.

Word List
tall
average height
short
blue
brown
blond
black
gray

What do you know?

A Listen and write.

Grace: I am _____tall_____.

Leo: I _____ Russian.

Tien: I have _____.

Isabel: I have _____ hair. I have _____ eyes.

Sandy: He _____ brown hair.

Paul: You _____ from Somalia.

Ben: We _____ brown eyes.

B Listen and fill in.

1. (A) I'm from Vietnam.   (B) I speak Vietnamese.

2. (A) Leo is divorced.   (B) Leo is single.

3. (A) Maria is from Mexico.   (B) Maria speaks Spanish.

4. (A) What is your zip code?   (B) What is your address?

C Talk about a classmate. Say, "Guess who."

Paul: **He** has **green** eyes. **He** has **gray** hair. He is **tall**. Guess who.

Grace: Is it **Leo**?

A: _____ has _____ eyes. _____ has _____ hair.
  (He/She)   (color)   (He/She)   (color)

_____ is _____ . Guess who.
 (He/She)

B: Is it _____?

32   **Unit 2**

D **Complete.**

| red | glasses | brown | ~~green~~ | short | tall |

1. Pete has _____green_____ eyes.

2. Pete has _____ hair.

3. Pete is _____.

4. Linda has _____ hair.

5. Linda has _____.

6. Linda is _____.

E ✔ **Check what you know.**

Learning Log

_____ address
_____ am
_____ are
_____ average height
_____ black
_____ blond
_____ blue
_____ Brazil
_____ brown
_____ China
_____ Chinese
_____ Colombia
_____ country
_____ divorced
_____ eighteen
_____ eleven
_____ eyes
_____ fifteen

_____ fourteen
_____ from
_____ glasses
_____ gray
_____ green
_____ hair
_____ has
_____ have
_____ identification form
_____ is
_____ language
_____ married
_____ Mexico
_____ middle initial
_____ nineteen
_____ Portuguese
_____ red
_____ Russia

_____ seventeen
_____ short
_____ single
_____ sixteen
_____ Somali
_____ Somalia
_____ Spanish
_____ speak
_____ tall
_____ thirteen
_____ twelve
_____ the United States
_____ Vietnam
_____ Vietnamese
_____ white
_____ widowed
_____ zip code

LOOKING BACK Look at page 18. What do you see? Tell a partner.

This is my family.

Who do you see?

1 Sandy Johnson's Family

 A **Listen.**

1. father

2. mother

3. brother

4. sister

5. daughter

6. son

Listen and repeat.

 B **Listen.**

Carlos: What's your **father's** name?
Sandy: His name is **Arthur**.
Carlos: What's your **mother's** name?
Sandy: Her name is **Ann**.

Listen and repeat.

C **Ask 4 classmates.**

A: What's your _____'s name?
B: His name is _____.
A: What's your _____'s name?
B: Her name is _____.

Word List

father
son
brother
mother
daughter
sister

2 Sandy's Family Tree

A Listen.

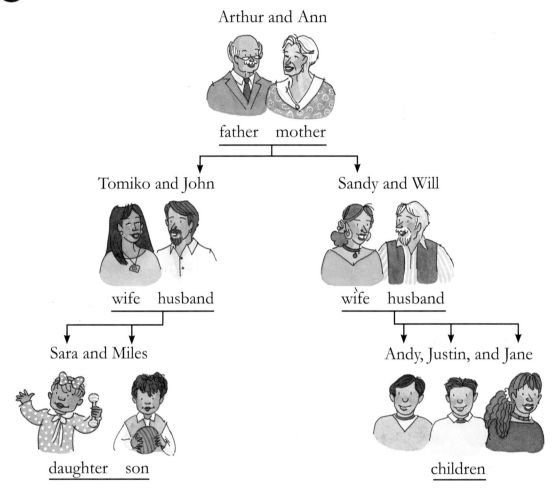

Arthur and Ann

father   mother

Tomiko and John

wife   husband

Sandy and Will

wife   husband

Sara and Miles

daughter   son

Andy, Justin, and Jane

children

Listen and repeat.

. . . .

B Listen and write.

1. **Sandy:** Arthur is my ___father___.   2. **John:**   Ann is my _____.

3. **Will:**   Sandy is my _____.   4. **Tomiko:** John is my _____.

5. **Sandy:** Justin is my _____.   6. **Will:**   Jane is my _____.

7. **John:**   Sara and Miles are my _____.

3 Who is that?

A **Listen.**

Isabel: Who is that?
Nadira: Sandy's **father**.

Listen and repeat.

B **Look at Sandy's family tree. Ask your partner.**

A: Who is that?
B: Sandy's _____ .

Word List

father
mother
husband
daughter
son

C **Fill in.**

1. **Who is Will?**

   Ⓐ Sandy's husband

   Ⓑ Sandy's brother

2. **Who is Andy?**

   Ⓐ Sandy's son

   Ⓑ Sandy's brother

3. **Who is Ann?**

   Ⓐ Sandy's mother

   Ⓑ Sandy's daughter

4. **Who is Jane?**

   Ⓐ Sandy's daughter

   Ⓑ Sandy's mother

MY LIFE **Draw your family tree.**

Talk in groups.

4 Carlos's Relatives

A Listen and read.

cousin   parents

aunt

Ricardo   Alfredo   Rudolfo   Magda
Celina

uncle

Umberto   Vera

grandfather   grandmother

Relatives = people in your family

Listen and repeat.

B Listen and circle.

1.

2.

3.

4.

5.

6.

7.

5 She is young.

 A **Listen and read.**

This is Ben's family.

1. Ben's grandfather is **old**.

2. His parents are **middle-aged**.

3. His sister is **young**.

B **Complete.**

1.

Leo's mother is _____old_____.

2.

Leo's granddaughter is _____.

3.

Leo's sisters are _____.

4.

Leo's father is _____.

C **Write about you.**

1. _____My grandfather_____ is old.

2. _____ is young.

3. _____ is middle-aged.

 A **Listen.**

1. Mr. and Mrs./Ms. Hancock

2. Mr. Hancock and Mrs./Ms. Tanaka

3. Miss/Ms. Lopez

Listen and repeat.

B **Write *Mr.*, *Ms.*, *Mrs.*, or *Miss*.**

1. __Mr.__ Danov

2. _____ Tanaka

3. _____ Lopez

4. _____ Lemat

Paul Lemat

7 Do you have children?

A **Listen.**

Paul: Do you have children?
Leo: Yes, I do. I have **three daughters**.
Tien: No, I don't.

Listen and repeat.

Word List

a daughter
daughters
a son
sons

B **Ask 5 classmates.**

A: Do you have children?
B: Yes, I do. I have _____ .
No, I don't.

C **Complete.**

children	do	don't	have	~~son~~

1. Andy is Sandy's _____son_____ .

2. Do you _____ a sister?

3. **A:** Do you have children?

   B: No, I _____ .

4. **A:** Do you have a daughter?

   B: Yes, I _____ .

5. Sandy and Will have three _____ .

8 How old are you?

Numbers

A Listen.

20 twenty	21 twenty-one	22 twenty-two	23 twenty-three	24 twenty-four	25 twenty-five
26 twenty-six	27 twenty-seven	28 twenty-eight	29 twenty-nine	30 thirty	40 forty
50 fifty	60 sixty	70 seventy	80 eighty	90 ninety	100 one hundred

Listen and repeat.

B Listen and write.

1. __28__ twenty-eight   2. _____ thirty   3. _____ ninety

4. _____ sixty   5. _____ fifty   6. _____ forty

7. _____ eighty   8. _____ seventy   9. _____ one hundred

C Listen.

Teacher: How old are you?
Student: I'm **21** years old.

Listen and repeat.

When you do not want to answer, say "I'd rather not say."

D Ask 5 classmates.

A: How old are you?
B: I'm _____ years old.

A Family Form

  A **Listen and read.**

Family Form

Your Name: Mr. Carlos Avila

Mr./Mrs./Ms. First and Last Name	Relative	Age
1. Mr. Umberto Avila	grandfather	69
2. Mrs. Vera Alves Avila	grandmother	63
3. Mr. Ricardo Avila	uncle	48
4. Ms. Celina Gomes Avila	aunt	42
5.		

B **Complete.**

Family Form

Your Name:

Mr./Mrs./Ms. First and Last Name	Relative	Age
1.		
2.		
3.		
4.		
5.		

10 Grammar: *Yes, I do. / No, I don't.*

 A **Listen and read.**

Listen and repeat.

 B **Listen and circle.**

1. (Yes, I do.)   No, I don't.   2. Yes, I do.   No, I don't.

3. Yes, I do.   No, I don't.   4. Yes, I do.   No, I don't.

C **Ask 8 classmates. Complete the chart.**

You: Do you have **a tall uncle**?
Carlos: Yes, I do.
You: Please sign here.

a tall uncle	a young husband	a middle-aged uncle
Carlos		
a son	two children	a grandfather
a brother	two sisters	two cousins

44   Unit 3

11 Grammar: *My, His, Her, Your, Their*

 A Listen and read.

My, His, Her, Your, Their

My name is Sandy.

His name is Paul.

Her name is Isabel.

Your name is Leo.

Their names are Nadira and Ben.

Listen and repeat.

 B Listen and circle.

1. His /(Her) name is Ann.
2. **His/Your** name is Will.
3. **My/Your** name is Tomiko.
4. **His/Her** name is Jane.

C Complete.

| Her | His | ~~My~~ | Their |

_____My_____ family is in Haiti. This is my father. _____

name is Franz. This is my mother. _____ name is Jaclin.

I have two sisters. _____ names are Jesi and Mariz.

12 Read: Nadira's Favorite Relative

 A **Listen and read.**

Nadira's Favorite Relative

Nadira's favorite relative is her grandmother. Her grandmother's name is Ubah. Ubah is short and old. She has brown eyes and white hair. Ubah is from Somalia. Now she lives in the United States. Ubah lives with Nadira. She lives with Nadira's three brothers, too.

Read with a partner.

B ✔ **Check. What is the story about?**

_____ **1.** Ubah is short and has brown eyes.

_____ **2.** Ubah is Nadira's favorite relative.

C **Circle.**

1. Ubah is **tall/short.**
2. Ubah has **black/white** hair.
3. Ubah lives in **Somalia/the United States.**
4. Ubah has four **grandchildren/brothers.**
5. Ubah is Nadira's **grandmother/sister.**

13 Write: My Family

A Complete.

family I ~~My~~	____My____ name is Maria Cruz. _____ am from Mexico. My _____ lives in the United States now.
children daughters son	I have three _____. I have one _____ and two _____.
four Their young	_____ names are Nestor, Ana, and Elena. My children are _____. I have _____ people in my family.

B Write about you.

My name is _____. I am from _____.

My family lives in _____ now.

I have _____

_____

_____.

I have _____ people in my family.

Read to a partner.

What do you know?

 A **Listen and fill in.**

1. My name is ____ Tanaka. (A) Mrs. (B) Ms.
2. I live at ____ Brown Road. (A) 60 (B) 16
3. I am ____. (A) single (B) married
4. My ____'s name is John. (A) husband (B) son
5. We have two ____. (A) children (B) classmates
6. My ____ has five children. (A) sister (B) brother

 B **Listen and fill in.**

1. (A) 16 (B) 60
2. (A) grandmother (B) grandfather
3. (A) Ms. Tanaka (B) Mr. Tanaka
4. (A) my (B) your
5. (A) His (B) Their

 C **Listen and circle.**

1. (80) 18 2. 70 60
3. 19 90 4. 25 20
5. 70 17 6. 20 12
7. 14 45 8. 15 50

D Write *Mr., Ms., Miss,* or *Mrs.*

1. Sandy is married. Her name is ___Mrs.___ Johnson.

2. Grace's husband is _____ Lee.

3. Isabel is single. She is _____ or _____ Lopez.

E Complete the chart. Write about your family.

Your Family	Name	Married, Single Divorced, Widowed
mother		
father		
sister		
brother		

F ✔ Check what you know.

Learning Log

____ aunt	____ grandmother	____ old
____ brother	____ have	____ one hundred
____ children	____ her	____ relative
____ cousin	____ his	____ seventy
____ daughter	____ husband	____ sister
____ do/don't	____ middle-aged	____ sixty
____ eighty	____ Miss	____ son
____ family	____ mother	____ their
____ father	____ Mr.	____ thirty
____ fifty	____ Mrs.	____ twenty
____ forty	____ Ms.	____ uncle
____ granddaughter	____ my	____ wife
____ grandfather	____ ninety	____ your

LOOKING BACK Look at page 34. What do you see? Tell a partner.

Review for Units 1–3

A Write *am*, *is,* or *are*.

PRESENT TENSE OF *BE*

I **am** tall.	We **are** tall. You **are** tall. They **are** tall.
He **is** tall. She **is** tall. It **is** tall.	

1. He _____is_____ tall.

2. They _____ old.

3. We _____ young.

4. She _____ short.

5. You _____ average height.

6. I _____ average height.

7. He and I _____ tall.

8. You _____ young.

9. You and I _____ middle-aged.

10. I _____ old.

B Write *have* or *has*.

PRESENT TENSE OF *HAVE*

I **have** blue eyes.	We **have** blue eyes. You **have** blue eyes. They **have** blue eyes.
He **has** blue eyes. She **has** blue eyes. It **has** blue eyes.	

1. Tien and Paul __have__ brown eyes.

2. Carlos _____ brown eyes.

3. You and I _____ black hair.

4. Will _____ gray hair.

5. My sister _____ brown eyes.

6. I _____ green eyes.

7. Isabel _____ blond hair.

8. They _____ black hair.

9. Ann _____ blue eyes.

10. We _____ red hair.

C Write about you.

1. My name _____is_____ _____ _____.

2. I _____ _____ eyes.

3. I _____ _____ hair.

4. I _____ from _____.

5. My teacher's name is _____ _____.

D Match.

1. __g__ What's your name?

2. ____ How do you spell that?

3. ____ Where are you from?

4. ____ What's your telephone number?

5. ____ What's your address?

6. ____ What's your zip code?

7. ____ What do you speak?

8. ____ What's your mother's name?

9. ____ What's your last name?

10. ____ What's your area code?

a. It's 5 Young Avenue.

b. C-A-R-L-O-S   A-V-I-L-A.

c. It's 90303.

d. I speak Portuguese.

e. Her name is Magda.

f. I'm from Brazil.

g. It's Carlos Avila.

h. It's (225) 555-5684.

i. It's 225.

j. It's Avila.

E Listen and circle.

1.

2.

3.

4.

Our Cultures: Greetings

A Write the words under the pictures.

bow	hug	kiss
say hello	~~shake hands~~	wave

shake hands

_____

_____

_____

_____   _____

B **Think about it. Complete the chart. How do people greet each other?**

| shake hands | hug | kiss |
| bow | wave | say hello |

| My native country | Both | Other countries |

bow

C **Talk in groups.**

In my country we hug. Everyone says hello. In some countries people bow.

Unit 4 Welcome to our house.

Where are the people?
Where is Sandy?

1 He's in the kitchen.

 A Listen.

1. kitchen

2. living room

3. bedroom

4. dining room

5. bathroom

6. backyard

Listen and repeat.

 B Listen.

Will: Where is **Justin**?
Sandy: **He's** in the **dining room**.
Will: Where are **Ann and Arthur**?
Sandy: They're in the **backyard**.

Listen and repeat.

Word List

Andy/bathroom
Jane/bedroom
Justin/dining room
Sandy and Will/kitchen

C Look at page 54. Talk with a partner.

A: Where is _____?
B: He's ⎪ in the _____.
　　 She's ⎪
A: Where are _____?
B: They're in the _____.

2 Is there a lamp in the bedroom?

  A **Listen.**

1. table   2. sofa   3. bed   4. lamp

5. air conditioner   6. fireplace   7. dresser   8. rug

Listen and repeat.

B **Listen.**

Carlos:	Is there a **fireplace** in the **living room**?
Man:	**Yes, there is.**
Carlos:	Is there a **rug** in the **bathroom**?
Man:	**No, there isn't.**

Listen and repeat.

C **Talk with a partner.**

A: Is there a _____ in the _____?
B: Yes, there is.
      No, there isn't.

Word List

lamp/living room
bed/bedroom
sofa/bedroom
dresser/bedroom

3

There's a shower in the bathroom.

 A **Listen.**

1. shower

2. sink

3. stove

4. window

5. microwave

6. closet

7. refrigerator

8. tub

Listen and repeat.

 B **Listen and circle.**

1. sink   (refrigerator)

2. sink   sofa

3. tub   shower

4. dresser   window

5. closet   air conditioner

6. microwave   refrigerator

MY LIFE   **Complete.**

Things in my kitchen	Things in my living room	Things in my bathroom

Talk in groups. Tell what is in your house.

There is a _____ in my _____.

4 Where do you live?

 A **Listen.**

1. I live in **a house**.   2. I live in **a rented room**.   3. I live in **an apartment**.

Listen and repeat.

B **Talk with 5 classmates.**

A: Where do you live?
B: I live in a | _____.
          an |

C **Complete. Work with a partner.**

~~an apartment~~   an apartment   a house   a rented room

1. _____ *an apartment* _____

2. _____

3. _____

4. _____

58   Unit 4

5 I need a refrigerator.

 A **Listen and read.**

Carlos's new apartment

Paul's garage

Carlos is happy with his new apartment. There is a bed and a dresser. There are four kitchen chairs. But Carlos needs a table. He needs other furniture, too. Paul has furniture for Carlos. The furniture is in Paul's garage.

 B **Listen.**

Paul:	What do you need?
Carlos:	I need a **table**.
Paul:	Do you need a **rug**?
Carlos:	No, I don't. Thanks.

Listen and repeat.

 C **Look at Activity A. Talk with a partner.**

Paul: What do you need?
Carlos: I need a _____ .
Paul: Do you need a _____ ?
Carlos: No, I don't. Thanks.

Word List

lamp
desk
dresser
refrigerator

Welcome to our house. 59

A ✔ Check.

Where do you…	eat?	cook?	shower?	sleep?	study?
living room					
kitchen					
dining room	✔				
bathroom					
bedroom					

B Listen and circle.

1.
2.
3.
4.

C Talk to a partner. Talk about your chart in Activity A.

Nadira: Where do you **eat**?
Ben: I eat in the **kitchen**. What about you?
Nadira: I **eat** in the **dining room**.

7 My Dream House

 A **Listen.**

1. in the city

2. in the country

3. at the beach

4. in the suburbs

Listen and repeat.

 B **Listen and read.**

Leo's Dream House

My dream house is in the city. There is a kitchen, a dining room, and a living room. My dream house has five bedrooms for my family. There are three bathrooms. I love my dream house.

MY LIFE   **Complete the sentences.**

1. My dream house is _____.

2. There is _____.

3. My dream house has _____.

4. There are _____.

5. I love my dream house.

Read your sentences to your group.

8 · 18 or 80?

 A **Listen.**

1. 12	20	2. 13	30	3. 14	40
4. 15	50	5. 16	60	6. 17	70
7. 18	80	8. 19	90		

Listen and repeat.

 B **Listen and circle.**

1. (60)	16	2. 19	90	3. 40	14
4. 18	80	5. 30	13	6. 17	70
7. 20	12	8. 15	50		

 C **Listen and write.**

1. My address is ___50___ Beach Street.

2. The house is _____ years old.

3. The rented room is at _____ Green Street.

4. There are _____ apartments.

5. There are _____ windows.

6. I have _____ tables.

7. We need _____ chairs in the dining room.

8. Ben has _____ pens.

9. The house has _____ rooms.

10. There are _____ lamps in the garage.

9 A Garage Sale

 A **Listen and read.**

Garage Sales

Americans love garage sales. There are books and furniture for sale. The books and furniture are good. But they are not new. Garage sales are fun.

 B **Listen and match.**

Sandy's students are at a garage sale. What do they need?

1. __b__ Isabel
2. _____ Carlos
3. _____ Ben
4. _____ Grace

a. a bike
b. a lamp
c. some CDs
d. a backpack

 C **Listen.**

Seller: What do you need?
Grace: I need a **bike**.
Seller: Good! I have a **bike** for sale.

Listen and repeat.

D **Talk with a partner.**

A: What do you need?
B: I need a _____.
A: Good! I have a _____ for sale.

Word List

backpack
bike
fan
pan
toaster

10 # Grammar: Singular and Plural Nouns

A Listen and read.

SINGULAR AND PLURAL NOUNS	
Singular	**Plural**
a sofa	two sofas
an air conditioner	four air conditioners

one city   five cities

city ⟶ cities

Listen and repeat.

B Listen and ✔ check.

1. ✔ apartment ____ apartments
2. ____ room ____ rooms
3. ____ kitchen ____ kitchens
4. ____ bedroom ____ bedrooms
5. ____ closet ____ closets
6. ____ shower ____ showers
7. ____ family ____ families
8. ____ seventy ____ seventies

C Write a singular or plural noun.

1. a dining room   two _____dining rooms_____

2. a closet   three _____

3. a _____ two dressers

4. a city   eight _____

5. a/an _____ ten _____

11 Grammar: Singular and Plural Nouns

A Circle the plural nouns.

Isabel likes tall (buildings.) She likes big cities. She lives in a rented room in a city. She has two chairs, a closet, and a dresser. Her pens are on the desk. There are two books on the dresser.

Isabel's parents and brothers live in a house. They live in the country. Their house has seven rooms. It has a kitchen, a dining room, a living room, and four bedrooms.

B Write singular or plural nouns.

1. three _____ **tables** _____
   (table)

2. two _____
   (bed)

3. a _____
   (fireplace)

4. three _____
   (lamp)

C Write *a* or *an*.

| Paul lives in **a** house. | Use **a** for one noun. |
| Maria lives in **an** apartment. | Use **an** before **a, e, i, o,** or **u.** |

I live in _a_ rented room. I want to live in ____ apartment. I need ____ kitchen, a living room, two bedrooms, and ____ bathroom. I need ____ apartment building with ____ backyard, too.

Welcome to our house.   65

12 Read: Tien's Apartment

 A **Listen and read.**

Tien's Apartment

Tien lives in an apartment building. The building has five floors. There are ten apartments on a floor.

Tien lives in apartment 305. It has a small living room, a small kitchen, and a small bedroom. It has a balcony, too. The balcony has flowers on it. Tien likes her building. She likes her apartment. But she loves her balcony.

Read with a partner.

B ✔ **Check.**

What is the story about?

_____ **1.** An apartment building   _____ **2.** Tien's apartment

C ✔ **Check Yes or No.**

	Yes	No
1. Tien lives in a house.		✔
2. Tien's building has 18 floors.		
3. Tien lives in apartment 503.		
4. Tien's apartment is small.		
5. Tien has flowers on her balcony.		

13 Write: A Note

A **Listen and read.**

Tien lives in Mr. Green's apartment building. She has a problem in her apartment. She writes a note to Mr. Green.

> Dear Mr. Green,
>   I live at 16 Beach Street.
> My apartment is 305. There is a
> broken window in the kitchen.
> Please fix the window. My telephone
> number is (337) 550-9764.
>   Thank you,
>   *Tien Lam*

B **Write about a problem.**

Dear _____,

   I live at _____. My apartment is _____.

There is a broken _____ in the _____.

Please fix the _____.

   My telephone number is _____.

                        Thank you,

                        _____

What do you know?

  A **Listen and circle.**

1. There is a sink in the _____. kitchen (bathroom)
2. There are books in the _____. bedroom garage
3. Paul lives in the _____. city suburbs
4. Nadira is _____. 13 30

B **Listen and fill in.**

1. (A) in the dining room (B) in an apartment
2. (A) a table (B) a lamp
3. (A) a pen (B) a rug
4. (A) a dresser (B) two dressers

C **Look at page 54. Complete the chart. Work with classmates.**

Room	Things in the Room
bathroom	shower, tub,
living room	
kitchen	

D Look at the picture. Complete.

| chairs | ~~kitchen~~ | stove | table |

This is Maria's ___kitchen___. It has a refrigerator, a sink, and a _____. There are four _____, too. Maria needs a _____.

E ✔ **Check what you know.**

Learning Log

____ air conditioner	
____ apartment	
____ backyard	
____ balcony	
____ bathroom	
____ beach	
____ bed	
____ bedroom	
____ bike	
____ building	
____ city	
____ closet	
____ cook	
____ dining room	
____ dream house	
____ dresser	

____ eat
____ fan
____ fireplace
____ floor
____ furniture
____ garage
____ garage sale
____ house
____ kitchen
____ lamp
____ living room
____ microwave
____ need
____ pan
____ refrigerator

____ rented room
____ rug
____ sale
____ shower
____ sink
____ sleep
____ small
____ sofa
____ stove
____ study
____ suburbs
____ table
____ toaster
____ tub
____ window

LOOKING BACK What do you see on page 54? Tell a partner.

Unit 5

I talk on the phone.

What's your name?
a b c d e f g
h　　n
u v

**Where are the people?
What do they do every day?**

What do you do every day?

A **Listen.**

Leo:	I read the newspaper.
Paul:	I work on my computer.
Andy:	I comb my hair.
Justin:	I brush my teeth.
Carlos:	I listen to music.
Maria:	I eat breakfast.
Sandy:	I talk on the phone.

Listen and repeat.

B **Listen and circle.**

1.     2.

3.     4.

C **Listen.**

Sandy:	What do you do every day?
Leo:	I **read the newspaper**.

Listen and repeat.

D **Talk with 5 classmates.**

A: What do you do every day?
B: I _____.

Word List

brush my teeth
eat breakfast
comb my hair
work on my computer

2 Days of the Week

 A **Listen.**

Sunday	Monday	Tuesday	Wednesday	Thursday	Friday	Saturday
	1	2	3	4	5	6
7	8	9	10	11	12	13

Listen and repeat.

 B **Listen and circle.**

1. Ben and Grace study on _____. ⬭Monday⬭ Tuesday
2. Leo cooks dinner on _____. Tuesday Thursday
3. Maria and Carlos go to garage sales on _____. Saturday Sunday
4. Nadira and Sandy watch TV on _____. Saturday Sunday

 C **Listen and complete.**

1. Paul plays soccer on _____Thursday_____.
2. Carlos and Ben go to school on _____.
3. Isabel and Grace go to garage sales on _____.
4. Leo and Maria go to class on _____.
5. Nadira cooks dinner on _____.

D **Ask 5 classmates.**

A: When do you study English?
B: I study English on _____.
A: When do you watch TV?
B: I watch TV on _____.

Word List

Monday
Tuesday
Wednesday
Thursday

3 Months

 A **Listen and read.**

January	February	March	April	May	June
July	August	September	October	November	December

Listen and repeat.

 B **Listen.**

Paul: When is your birthday?
Isabel: It's in **October**.

Listen and repeat.

C **Talk with 7 classmates.**

A: When is your birthday?
B: It's in _____.

D **Write.**

Apr.	Aug.	Dec.	Feb.	~~Jan.~~	Jul.
Jun.	May	Mar.	Nov.	Oct.	Sept.

1. January = ___Jan.___   2. February = _____

3. March = _____   4. April = _____

5. May = _____   6. June = _____

7. July = _____   8. August = _____

9. September = _____   10. October = _____

11. November = _____   12. December = _____

4 What time is it?

 A Listen.

1. 10:00

2. 7:15

3. 1:45

4. 3:30

5. 2:00

6. 4:45

7. 12:30

8. 8:15

9. 9:20

Listen and repeat.

 B Listen.

Nadira: What time is it?
Leo: It's **10:00**.

Listen and repeat.

For: 10:00

Say:
  It's ten o'clock.
or
  It's ten.

C Look at the clocks. Talk with a partner.

A: What time is it?
B: It's _____.

74 Unit 5

A Listen.

1. 6:00

2. 8:15

3. 3:30

4. 5:45

Listen and repeat.

 B Listen and circle.

1. (6:30)	7:30	**2.**	8:30	8:45
3. 12:15	12:45	**4.**	2:00	2:15
5. 4:00	5:00	**6.**	9:15	9:45

C Write about you. Read your sentences in groups.

1. I get up at ____6:00____.

2. I go to school at _____.

3. I go to work at _____.

4. I eat lunch at _____.

5. I go home at _____.

6. I go to bed at _____.

I talk on the phone. 75

Making an Appointment

 A **Listen.**

Grace: I'd like to make an appointment for a **haircut**.
Woman: Can you come on Friday at **11:45**?
Grace: Friday at **11:45**? That's fine.

Listen and repeat.

B **Talk with a partner.**

checkup/1:15

tune-up/3:30

haircut/11:45

A: I'd like to make an appointment for a _____.
B: Can you come on Friday at _____?
A: Friday at _____? That's fine.

  C **Listen and write the times.**

NOVEMBER						
Sunday	Monday	Tuesday	Wednesday	Thursday	Friday	Saturday
12	13 haircut 5:30	14	15 tune-up ____	16	17 checkup ____	18

7 How often do you study?

 A **Listen and read.**

NOVEMBER						
Sunday	**Monday**	**Tuesday**	**Wednesday**	**Thursday**	**Friday**	**Saturday**
			study 1 shop for food	study 2	study 3	study 4
study 5	study 6	study 7	study 8 shop for food	study 9	study 10	study 11
study 12	study 13	study 14	study 15 shop for food	study 16	study 17	study 18 get a haircut
study 19	study 20	study 21	study 22	study 23	study 24	study 25

1. I study English **every day**.

2. I shop for food **once a week**.

3. I get a haircut **once a month**.

 B **Listen.**

Sandy: What do you do once a week?
Will: I get a haircut.
Tien: I go to garage sales.
Carlos: I cook dinner.

Listen and repeat.

MY LIFE **Complete. Read your sentences to your group.**

Once a day I _____.

Once a week I _____.

Once a month I _____.

I talk on the phone. 77

8 Ordinal Numbers

 A **Listen.**

1st first	2nd second	3rd third	4th fourth	5th fifth	6th sixth	7th seventh
8th eighth	9th ninth	10th tenth	11th eleventh	12th twelfth	13th thirteenth	14th fourteenth

Listen and repeat.

B **Write the number.**

1. 14th fourteenth   2. _____ twelfth   3. _____ fifth   4. _____ seventh

5. _____ third   6. _____ first   7. _____ second   8. _____ ninth

 C **Listen and circle.**

1. (5th)   15th   2. 3rd   13th

3. 2nd   12th   4. 4th   14th

5. 3rd   13th   6. 1st   11th

 D **Listen.**

Teacher   What is your date of birth?
Student: March 16, 1980.

Listen and repeat.

For: 2001

Say: two thousand one

E **Ask 7 classmates.**

A: What is your date of birth?
B: _____.

A Read.

Medical History

Hilltop Health Clinic (323) 555-4567

Lee	Grace	--	3/16/80
Last Name	First Name	MI	Date of Birth

B Complete the form.

For: 3/16/80

Say: March 16th, 1980

Medical History

Hilltop Health Clinic (323) 555-4567

Last Name	First Name	MI	Date of Birth

MY LIFE   Write the date of birth for 5 relatives.

1. Grandmother   9/6/45
2. _____   _____
3. _____   _____
4. _____   _____
5. _____   _____
6. _____   _____

My grandmother's date of birth is September 6, 1945.

Talk in groups.

Grammar: Simple Present Tense

  A **Listen and read.**

SIMPLE PRESENT TENSE		
I	**take**	photos.
He	**takes**	photos.
She	**takes**	photos.
It	**takes**	photos.
We	**take**	photos.
You	**take**	photos.
They	**take**	photos.

Listen and repeat.

  B **Listen and circle.**

1. She **take** /**takes** photos.

2. It **eat** / **eats** cake.

3. We **say** / **says** "Happy Birthday."

4. I **open** / **opens** my presents.

5. Paul **call** / **calls** Isabel on the phone.

11 Grammar: Simple Present Tense

A Complete.

| combs | eats | gets | ~~have~~ | reads | talk | work |

1. Will and Sandy ____have____ breakfast at 7:30 A.M.

2. Will _____ his hair every morning.

3. He _____ a haircut once a month.

4. I _____ on my computer every day.

5. Leo _____ the newspaper every morning.

6. We _____ on the phone once a week.

7. My dog _____ every morning.

Review: Present Tense Be

I	am	we	are
he	is	you	are
she	is	they	are
it	is		

B Write am, is, or are.

1. **Tien:** You ____are____ happy today.

   Isabel: Yes. I _____. It _____ my birthday.

2. **Leo:** Hi. Is Ben at home?

   Grace: Yes, he _____ in the living room.

3. **Will:** Where are Ann and Arthur?

   Sandy: They _____ in the backyard.

4. **Justin:** What time is it?

   Andy: It _____ 8:15. We _____ late for school.

Read with a partner.

C Write.

I _____ a student.

My classmate _____ lunch at noon.

My family and I _____ on the weekend.

Read: Happy Birthday

 A **Listen and read.**

Happy Birthday

It's May 10. Today is Isabel's birthday. She is 21 years old. Tien, Ben, Grace, and Carlos visit Isabel's house at 2:30 in the afternoon. Isabel takes photos of her classmates. They eat cake and say, "Happy Birthday." Isabel opens presents. She says, "Thank you." It's a great day!

Read with a partner.

B **Circle.**

1. It's May 10.   It's May 21.

2. Isabel is 21.   Isabel is 12.

3. It is Ben's birthday.   It is Isabel's birthday.

4. They open presents.   They eat cake.

5. Isabel says, "Happy Birthday."   Isabel says, "Thank you."

6. The party is at 2:30.   The class is at 2:30.

13 Write: An Email

A Complete.

| ~~are~~ | Birthday | eat | give | say | are |

Dear Mom and Dad,

These _____*are*_____ the photos from my birthday party with my classmates. _____ parties in the United States _____ very nice. People _____ gifts and _____ cake. They also _____, "Happy Birthday."

Love, Isabel

B Write about Isabel. What does Isabel do at the party?

1. Isabel _____.

2. Isabel _____.

3. Isabel _____.

What do you know?

 A **Listen and write.**

1. My birthday is ___October___ 12.
2. Paul's birthday is _____ 4.
3. My class is at _____.
4. I study on _____.

 B **Listen and fill in.**

1. Ⓐ Ben is Chinese.   Ⓑ Ben speaks Chinese.
2. Ⓐ Leo writes the newspaper.   Ⓑ Leo reads the newspaper.
3. Ⓐ We talk on the phone.   Ⓑ Carlos and Maria talk on the phone.
4. Ⓐ You eat breakfast every day.   Ⓑ They eat breakfast every day.
5. Ⓐ Sandy and Will cook dinner.   Ⓑ Jane cooks dinner.
6. Ⓐ It's ten o'clock.   Ⓑ It's October 10.
7. Ⓐ Leo's birthday is September 3.   Ⓑ Leo's birthday is September 30.
8. Ⓐ Nadira has class on Tuesday.   Ⓑ Nadira has class on Thursday.

 C **Listen and circle.**

1. (7:00)   7th   2. 6th   6:30
3. 10th   11th   4. 2:00   2:30
5. 13th   30th   6. 9:45   5:45
7. 8:00   8th   8. 3:00   3rd
9. 15th   50   10. 13th   30th

D **Ask 5 classmates.**

1. What do you do every day?
2. When is your birthday?
3. When do you go to school?
4. What do you do once a month?

E **Listen and write.**

| 6:00 | 8:00 A.M. | April | ~~Monday~~ |

Checkup Appointment
On: <u>Monday</u>,
_____ 21, at _____
Edward J. Weiss, D.D.S.
517 Old Road

Jane's Haircuts
Tuesday to Saturday
9:30 A.M. to _____ P.M.
310 Cook Road

F ✔ **Check the words you know.**

Learning Log

___ appointment	___ February	___ newspaper	___ start
___ April	___ fifth	___ ninth	___ study
___ August	___ first	___ November	___ Sunday
___ birthday	___ fourteenth	___ o'clock	___ teeth
___ breakfast	___ fourth	___ October	___ tenth
___ brush	___ Friday	___ often	___ third
___ call	___ give	___ once a month	___ thirteenth
___ checkup	___ haircut	___ once a week	___ Thursday
___ cleaning	___ home	___ party	___ time
___ clock	___ January	___ people	___ Tuesday
___ comb	___ July	___ phone	___ tune-up
___ date of birth	___ June	___ play	___ TV
___ December	___ listen	___ Saturday	___ twelfth
___ dinner	___ lunch	___ second	___ watch
___ eat	___ March	___ September	___ Wednesday
___ eighth	___ May	___ seventh	___ week
___ eleventh	___ Monday	___ shop	___ work
___ every day	___ movie	___ sixth	

LOOKING BACK Who do you see on page 70? Tell a partner.

Unit 6 — Let's go shopping.

Where are the students?
What do you see?

1 I'm looking for a coat.

  A **Listen.**

1. a shirt

2. a coat

3. a sweater

4. shoes

5. a watch

6. a dress

7. pants

8. a suit

Listen and repeat.

 B **Listen.**

Isabel: Excuse me. I'm looking for **a sweater**.
Clerk: Follow me, please.
Isabel: Thank you.

Listen and repeat.

C **Talk with a partner.**

A: Excuse me. I'm looking for _____.
B: Follow me, please.
A: Thank you.

Word List

a coat
a dress
a shirt
a sweater
pants
shoes

2 **May I help you?**

 A **Listen.**

1. a blouse

2. a bathing suit

3. a skirt

4. a belt

5. a jacket

6. a cap

7. socks

8. a scarf

Listen and repeat.

 B **Listen.**

Clerk: May I help you?
Carlos: Yes, I need **a bathing suit.**

Listen and repeat.

Word List

a bathing suit
a skirt
a cap
socks

C **Talk with a partner.**

A: May I help you?
B: Yes, I need _____.

D **Complete.**

1. Nadira needs a _____.

2. Ben and Carlos need _____.

What color is your jacket?

 A Listen.

white   black   brown   pink   red   orange   yellow   green   blue   purple

Listen and repeat.

 **B** Listen and circle.

1.    2.

3.   4.

5.   6.

 C Listen.

Sandy: What color is your **jacket**?
Grace: Green.
Sandy: What color are your **shoes**?
Grace: Yellow.

Listen and repeat.

D Talk with a partner about clothes.

A: What color is your _____ ?
            are

B: _____ .
  (Color)

Word List

dress
shirt
pants
shoes

4 What are you wearing?

 A **Listen.**

Grace: What are you wearing to the party?
Maria: I'm wearing a **blue dress**. What is Ben wearing?
Grace: He's wearing a **brown suit**.

Listen and repeat.

B **Talk with 3 classmates.**

A: What are you wearing?

B: I'm wearing a ⎱ _____ _____ .
       an ⎰   (color)   (clothing)

Word List

blue
brown
green
dress
jacket
shirt

C **Talk with a partner. Look at the picture on page 86.**

A: What is _____ wearing?
              (name)

B: He's ⎱ wearing (a/an) _____ _____ .
       She's ⎰   (color)   (clothing)

MY LIFE **Complete the sentences.**

I wear ___a bathing suit___ to the beach.   I wear _____ to work.
I wear _____ to school.   I wear _____ to parties.

Read your sentences to your group.

5 What's your favorite color?

A **Listen.**

Nadira: What's your favorite color?
Leo: Brown. What's your favorite color?
Nadira: Orange.

Listen and repeat.

B **Talk with a partner.**

A: What's your favorite color?
B: _____. What's your favorite color?
A: _____.

C **Ask classmates.**

You: What's your favorite color?
Leo: Brown.
You: Please sign here.

brown Leo	orange	blue
yellow	black	red
purple	pink	green
brown	orange	blue
yellow	black	red
purple	pink	green

  **A** **Listen.**

1. small
(S)

2. medium
(M)

3. large
(L)

Listen and repeat.

 B **Listen and circle.**

1. small   medium   (large)   2. small   medium   large

3. small   medium   large   4. small   medium   large

5. small   medium   large   6. small   medium   large

7. small   medium   large   8. small   medium   large

 C **Listen.**

Clerk: What size are you?
Leo: I'm a **large**.

Listen and repeat.

D **Talk with 5 classmates.**

A: What size are you?
B: I'm a _____.

7 The jacket is too small.

 A Listen.

1. too short   **2.** too long   **3.** too small   **4.** too big

Listen and repeat.

B Look at Activity A. Match.

1. _b_ Paul's pants   **a.** is too small.

2. ____ Maria's pants   **b.** are too short.

3. ____ Tien's jacket   **c.** is too big.

4. ____ Carlos's shirt   **d.** are too long.

C Write 3 sentences about Leo's clothes.

1. _____.

2. _____.

3. _____.

Money

Numbers

 A **Listen.**

1. a penny
1 cent (1¢)

2. a nickel
5 cents (5¢)

3. a dime
10 cents (10¢)

4. a quarter
25 cents (25¢)

Listen and repeat.

 B **Listen.**

1. 1 dollar
$1.00

2. 5 dollars
$5.00

3. 10 dollars
$10.00

4. 20 dollars
$20.00

Listen and repeat.

C **Write how much.**

1.

94 Unit 6

A Check

Community

A Read.

Isabel is buying a sweater at Spring Department Store. The sweater is $26.25. She is writing a check.

```
                                                           1179
Isabel Lopez
102 E 21st Street
Lakeland, CA 95555              DATE Nov. 19, 2010  2-5654-1234

PAY
TO THE     Spring Department Store        $   26.25
ORDER OF
          Twenty-six and 25/100                 DOLLARS

Lakeland
City Bank
MEMO    sweater                    Isabel Lopez
     "012345" ":123456543":01234567"
```

B Write a check.

You are buying shoes at Spring Department Store. The shoes are $47.25.

```
                                                           1179
                                                    2-5654-1234
                               DATE_____

PAY
TO THE     _____        $ _____
ORDER OF
          _____     DOLLARS

Lakeland
City Bank
MEMO    _____    _____
     "012345" ":123456543":01234567"
```

10 Grammar: Adjectives and Nouns

  A **Listen and read.**

ADJECTIVES AND NOUNS		
Adjectives	**Nouns**	**Examples**
white	blouse	She has a **white blouse**.
short	skirt	She has a **short skirt**.
big	hat	She has a **big hat**.
red	shoes	She has **red shoes**.

Listen and repeat.

B **Look at the picture. Complete the sentences.**

big	red	~~white~~	blue	long

1. Andy is wearing _____white_____ shoes.

2. Andy and Justin are wearing _____ pants.

3. Justin is wearing a _____ shirt.

4. Justin is wearing a _____ cap.

5. Andy and Justin have a _____ book.

C **Talk about a classmate.**

_____ is wearing a/an _____ _____ and _____ _____.
(Name)   (adjective)   (noun)   (adjective)   (noun)

11 Grammar: Adjectives and Nouns

 A Listen.

Listen and repeat.

B Read. Look at Activity A. Match.

__h__ 1. large   **a.** suit

____ 2. brown   **b.** dress

____ 3. black   **c.** jacket

____ 4. purple   **d.** boots

____ 5. pink   **e.** skirt

____ 6. blue   **f.** shoes

____ 7. red   **g.** blouse

____ 8. yellow   **h.** hat

____ 9. green   **i.** sweater

C Look at Activity A. Write.

1. a ____large____ ____hat____   2. a _____ _____

3. a _____ _____   4. a _____ _____

5. a _____ _____   6. a _____ _____

7. a _____ _____   8. _____ _____

Let's go shopping. 97

Read: A Catalog

 A Listen and read.

A.
CHILDREN'S PANTS
Sizes: small, medium, large
Colors: blue, red, or brown
Price: $18.75

23 | catalog shopping

B.
WOMEN'S SWEATERS & SKIRTS

Women's Sweaters
Sweater sizes:
small, medium, large
Sweater colors:
green or red
Price: $22.00

Women's Skirts
Skirt sizes:
small, medium, large.
Skirt colors:
brown, green, or blue
Price: $22.95

C.
MEN'S SUITS
Sizes: small, medium, large, extra large
Colors: brown, black, or blue
Price: $62.50

Read with a partner.

B Look at Activity A. Write the answers.

1. How much are the men's suits? $62.50

2. What colors are the sweaters? _____

3. What sizes are the children's pants? _____

4. How much are the skirts? _____

5. What colors are the men's suits? _____

A **Complete Sandy's shopping list.**

Price: $10.00   **Price:** $12.50   **Price:** $9.75   **Price:** $20.00   **Price:** $22.00

Shopping List

1. Justin: a ____blue____ baseball cap   Size medium $10.00
   (color)

2. Andy: white _____   Size 7 $_____
   (clothing)

3. Jane: a _____ sweater   Size small $9.75
   (color)

4. Will: a green _____   Size large $20.00
   (clothing)

5. Sandy: a long _____ skirt   Size medium $_____
   (color)

What do you know?

 A **Listen and match.**

_____ _____ _____ 1

 B **Listen and fill in.**

1. Ⓐ I'm a small.   Ⓑ I'm a medium.

2. Ⓐ He's wearing a sweater.   Ⓑ He's wearing shoes.

3. Ⓐ It's a black suit.   Ⓑ It's a brown suit.

4. Ⓐ It's $13.25.   Ⓑ It's $30.25.

C **Talk about a classmate. Say, "Guess who."**

Leo: She's wearing **a white shirt** and **green pants**.
          Guess who.
Sandy: Is it **Isabel**?
Leo: No. Guess again.
Sandy: Is it **Maria**?
Leo: Yes! Your turn.

D **Write about you.**

1. What are you wearing today? _____

2. What do you wear to parties? _____

3. What do you wear to the beach? _____

E Read.

At home, Carlos loves to wear his brown sweater, blue pants, and white socks.

Write about your favorite clothes.

At home, _____

_____

_____

_____.

- -

F ✔ Check what you know.

Learning Log

____ bathing suit	____ favorite	____ red
____ belt	____ green	____ scarf
____ big	____ help	____ shirt
____ black	____ jacket	____ shoes
____ blouse	____ large	____ shopping list
____ blue	____ long	____ short
____ brown	____ medium	____ size
____ cap	____ money	____ skirt
____ catalog	____ nickel	____ small
____ cent	____ orange	____ socks
____ clothes	____ pants	____ suit
____ coat	____ penny	____ sweater
____ color	____ pink	____ watch
____ dime	____ price	____ wear
____ dollar	____ purple	____ white
____ dress	____ quarter	____ yellow

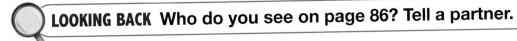

LOOKING BACK Who do you see on page 86? Tell a partner.

A Circle the plural nouns.

SINGULAR AND PLURAL NOUNS

	Singular	Plural
Most nouns	a coat a room	two coat**s** four room**s**
Nouns that end in -ch, -sh, -s, -x, -z	a wat**ch** a dress	12 wat**ches** 200 dres**ses**

Isabel lives in a rented room. She has a closet, a dresser and two (chairs.) Her dresses and coats are in the closet. There are two watches on the dresser.

Isabel's family lives in a house. Their house has seven rooms. It has a kitchen, a dining room, a living room, four bedrooms, and two bathrooms.

B Complete.

SIMPLE PRESENT TENSE

I You We They	**read** books. **speak** English. **eat** breakfast. **work** every day.	He She It	**reads** books. **speaks** English. **eats** breakfast.

1. (read)   I _____ read _____ the newspaper every day.

2. (work)   Maria _____ on a computer once a week.

3. (play)   Justin and Andy _____ soccer on Saturday.

4. (eat)   Paul _____ breakfast every day.

5. (cook)   We _____ dinner on Thursday.

6. (talk)   Sandy _____ on the phone every day.

7. (need)   Tien and Grace _____ books.

8. (sleep)   They _____ in the bedroom.

9. (speak)   I _____ Spanish.

10. (live)   He _____ at 11 Green Street.

C Match.

1. __C__ Where do you live?
2. _____ What do you need?
3. _____ Where's the refrigerator?
4. _____ What's she wearing?
5. _____ When is your birthday?
6. _____ What time is it?

a. She's wearing a red dress.

b. It's 10:45.

c. I live in an apartment.

d. It's in the kitchen.

e. I need a desk.

f. It's in June.

D Read.

Maria is buying a sweater and shirts on the Internet. This is the checkout page.

Ship To: Maria Cruz
115 Brown Road
Los Angeles, CA 90037

Item	How many?	Size	Color	Price	Subtotal
sweater	1	small	black	$28.95	$28.95
shirt	3	medium	white	$11.35	$34.05

Subtotal	$63.00
Shipping & Handling	$4.95
Total: $67.95	

E ✔ Check Yes or No.

	Yes	No
1. Maria is buying a sweater and three shirts.	✔	_____
2. The sweater is black.	_____	_____
3. Maria needs a medium sweater.	_____	_____
4. The shirts are large.	_____	_____
5. Maria's address is 115 Brown Road.	_____	_____

A Circle the types of houses. <u>Underline</u> the countries.

A (pole house) in <u>Myanmar</u>

An adobe house in Morocco

An apartment building in Japan

A Victorian house in the US

A yurt in Mongolia

A palazzo in Italy

B Think about it. Complete the chart. What is your home like?

Types of houses	
In my native country	**In the USA**
 house	

C Talk in groups.

In my native country my house is in the suburbs. In the US my apartment is in the city. In my native country, my house has 4 bedrooms, a kitchen, a living room, and a big backyard. My apartment has one bedroom, a kitchen, a living room, and a small balcony.

Unit 7
I'm so hungry!

What food do you see?

We need eggs.

 A **Listen.**

1. eggs

2. ice cream

3. carrots

4. apples

5. potatoes

6. milk

7. rice

8. beef

9. bananas

Listen and repeat.

B **Listen.**

Carlos: We need some **eggs**.
Antonio: That's right. We need some **apples**, too.

Listen and repeat.

C **Talk with 5 classmates.**

A: We need some _____.
B: That's right. We need some _____, too.

Word List

carrots
potatoes
bananas
beef

I'm so hungry! 107

2 Do we need some fish?

 A **Listen.**

1. cake   2. bread   3. fish   4. chicken   5. lettuce

6. oranges   7. butter   8. cheese   9. pasta   10. beans

Listen and repeat.

 B **Listen.**

Grace: Do we need some **butter**?
Ben: **Yes, we do.**
Grace: Do we need some **oranges**?
Ben: **No, we don't.**

Listen and repeat.

Word List

potatoes
oranges
cheese
eggs
fish

C **Talk with 5 classmates.**

A: Do we need some _____?
B: |Yes, we do.
   |No, we don't.

3 I'm looking for some apples.

 A Listen.

| Aisle 1 PRODUCE | Aisle 2 MEAT | Aisle 3 BAKERY | Aisle 4 DAIRY |

Grace: Excuse me. I'm looking for some apples.
Clerk: Apples are in aisle 1.
Grace: I'm looking for bread, too.
Clerk: Bread is in aisle 3.

Listen and repeat.

Produce =
Fruits and
Vegetables

 B Listen and complete the chart.

Food	Aisle 1 Produce	Aisle 2 Meat	Aisle 3 Bakery	Aisle 4 Dairy
1. apples	✔			
2. beef				
3. chicken				
4. cheese				
5. cake				
6. milk				
7. lettuce				

I eat three meals a day.

 A **Listen.**

1. breakfast   2. lunch   3. dinner

Listen and repeat.

 **B** **Listen.**

NOVEMBER

Sunday	Monday	Tuesday	Wednesday	Thursday	Friday	Saturday
12	13	14	15	16	17	18
milk	milk	milk	milk	milk	milk	milk
cereal	cereal	cereal	cereal	cereal	eggs	cereal

Leo: What do you have for **breakfast**?
Ben: I always have **milk**. I usually have **cereal**. I sometimes have **eggs**.

Listen and repeat.

C **Talk with 5 classmates.**

A: What do you have for _____?
B: I always have _____. I usually have _____. I sometimes have _____.

5 Let's have lunch.

A Listen.

Leo: It's **12:30**. I'm so hungry!
Maria: Me, too. Let's have **lunch**.
Leo: What do you want?
Maria: **A chicken sandwich**. And you?
Leo: **Sushi**.

Listen and repeat.

B Talk with 3 classmates.

A: It's _____. I'm so hungry!
B: Me, too. Let's have _____.
A: What do you want?
B: _____. And you?
A: _____.

Word List

7:30/breakfast/an egg/cereal
1:30/lunch/a taco/soup
6:30/dinner/rice/vegetables

C Complete. Read to your group.

I usually have breakfast at ___6:00___. Then I have lunch at _____.
                                          (time)   (time)

I have dinner at _____. I sometimes have _____ for dinner.
                            (time)   (food)

MY LIFE Complete the chart. Write the food you usually eat.

Breakfast	Lunch	Dinner
eggs		

Tell your group what food you usually eat.

6 A tuna sandwich, please.

A Listen.

Server:	May I help you?
Paul:	Yes, **a tuna sandwich**, please.
Server:	Anything to drink today?
Paul:	Yes, thanks. Some **coffee**, please.

Listen and repeat.

B Ask 4 classmates.

A: May I help you?
B: Yes, _____, please.
A: Anything to drink today?
B: Yes, thanks. Some _____, please.

Word List

a hamburger
a tuna sandwich
pizza
coffee
tea
soda

C Circle what's in the sandwich.

bread	cake	cheese
fish	lettuce	oranges
rice	tomatoes	tuna

7 Do you have eggs for lunch?

A **Listen.**

Isabel:	Do you have **eggs** for **lunch**?
Nadira:	Yes, I do.
Paul:	No, I don't.

Listen and repeat.

B **Talk with 6 classmates.**

A: Do you have _____ for _____ ?
B: Yes, I do.
Sometimes.
No, I don't.

Word List

eggs/breakfast
chicken/dinner
pasta/lunch
fish/dinner

C **Write 3 questions.**

1. ___Do___ you have _____ for breakfast?

2. _____ _____ have _____ for lunch?

3. _____ _____ _____ _____ for dinner?

Ask a classmate.

MY LIFE **Write.**

1. I always have _____ for breakfast.

2. I sometimes have _____ for lunch.

3. I don't have _____ for dinner.

Read your sentences to your group.

Containers

  **A** Listen.

1. a bottle

2. a can

a bag

3. a bag

4. a box

5. a carton

6. a jar

Listen and repeat.

 B Listen and circle.

1. (a box)	a bottle	2. a bag	a jar
3. a bottle	a can	4. a carton	a bottle
5. a jar	a box	6. a bottle	a can

C Look at the picture. Complete the shopping list.

Shopping List
a box of cereal

9 A Potluck Dinner

 A **Listen and read.**

A Potluck Dinner

Once a month Sandy's class has a potluck dinner. Sandy brings coffee, milk, and tea. The students bring different foods. They bring fruit, vegetables, or meat. Carlos always brings ice cream. It's his favorite dessert. Sandy's students make special foods from their countries. The potluck dinners are fun, and the food is interesting.

Read with a partner.

B ✔ **Check *True* or *False*.**

	True	False
1. Sandy's class has a potluck dinner once a month.	✔	
2. Sandy brings soda to the potluck dinners.		
3. All the students bring desserts.		
4. Ice cream is Carlos's favorite dessert.		
5. The students bring foods from their countries.		
6. The potluck lunches are fun.		

C **Write about you.**

Your class has a potluck dinner. What food do you bring?

Food: _____

Grammar: Count Nouns

  A **Listen and read.**

COUNT NOUNS			
Singular		**Plural (-s or -es)**	
one egg an egg		egg**s** some egg**s**	
one sandwich a sandwich		three sandwich**es** some sandwich**es**	

Listen and repeat.

  B **Listen and circle.**

1. (orange)   oranges   2. potato   potatoes

3. banana   bananas   4. dessert   desserts

5. box   boxes   6. apple   apples

7. pie   pies   8. lunch   lunches

Add -es to words ending in ch, o, sh, s, x, or z.

C **Circle.**

1. This is an **(egg)/eggs**.

2. Do you need four **box/boxes**?

3. I want some **banana/bananas**.

4. Nestor brings a **lunch/lunches**.

5. Paul brings some **orange/oranges** to the potluck.

6. Sandy brings a **carton/cartons** of milk to the potluck.

116 Unit 7

Grammar: Non-count Nouns

A Listen and read.

NON-COUNT NOUNS

Milk **is** white.

Cereal **is** brown.

Non-count nouns are always singular.

Listen and repeat.

B Read and ✔ check.

	Count	Non-count
1. Sandy likes **coffee** in the morning.		✔
2. She likes an **egg** for breakfast, too.		
3. Leo likes **rice** for lunch.		
4. He likes **fish**, too.		
5. Grace and Ben like **beef** for dinner.		
6. They like **potatoes**, too.		

C ✔ Check. Write the plural for count nouns.

Noun	Count	Non-count
box	✔ boxes	
coffee		
lunch		
oil		
pasta		

 A **Listen and read.**

Maria wants good food for her family. She wants to save money, too. She uses coupons to save money.

Read with a partner.

B **Write.**

Cereal	Apple Juice	Beans
Price: $4.29	Price: _____	Price: _____
Coupon: $1.00	Coupon: _____	Coupon: _____
Cost: $3.29	Cost: _____	Cost: _____

13 Write: A Shopping List

A Listen and read.

Paul likes to cook dinner for his friends. This is his shopping list.

4 tomatoes
lettuce
beef
a carton of milk
2 bottles of soda
6 eggs
butter

B Write a shopping list for a dinner party.

Shopping List

I'm so hungry! 119

What do you know?

 A **Listen and fill in the answer sheet.**

1. **A.** chicken   **B.** bread
2. **A.** hamburger   **B.** milk
3. **A.** apples   **B.** juice
4. **A.** oranges   **B.** eggs
5. **A.** beef   **B.** cheese

ANSWER SHEET

1. (A) (B)
2. (A) (B)
3. (A) (B)
4. (A) (B)
5. (A) (B)

 B **Listen and fill in the answer sheet.**

1. **A.** Let's have lunch.   **B.** Let's have hamburgers.
2. **A.** Do we need fruit?   **B.** Do we need fish?
3. **A.** What about you?   **B.** What do we need?
4. **A.** Excuse me.   **B.** May I help you?
5. **A.** Do you have eggs for lunch?   **B.** Anything to drink today?
6. **A.** Do we need two boxes of cereal?   **B.** Do we need a box of cereal?

ANSWER SHEET

1. (A) (B)
2. (A) (B)
3. (A) (B)
4. (A) (B)
5. (A) (B)
6. (A) (B)

C **Ask 5 classmates.**

You: What is your favorite food?
Carlos: Ice cream.

Classmate	Favorite Food
Carlos	ice cream

D Look at the picture. Tell a partner what food you need.

A: What do you need?
B: I need _____.

F ✔ Check what you know.

Learning Log

____ aisle	____ can	____ hamburger	____ pizza
____ always	____ carrot	____ hungry	____ potato
____ apple	____ carton	____ ice cream	____ potluck
____ bag	____ cereal	____ jar	____ produce
____ bakery	____ cheese	____ lettuce	____ rice
____ banana	____ chicken	____ lunch	____ sandwich
____ beans	____ coffee	____ meal	____ soda
____ beef	____ container	____ meat	____ sometimes
____ bottle	____ coupon	____ milk	____ sugar
____ box	____ dairy	____ oil	____ taco
____ bread	____ dessert	____ orange	____ tea
____ breakfast	____ dinner	____ pasta	____ tuna
____ butter	____ egg	____ peanut butter	____ usually
____ cake	____ fish		____ vegetable

LOOKING BACK What do you see on page 106? Tell a partner.

Unit 8

How's the weather?

Where's Carlos?
Where's Tien?

1 It's raining.

A Listen.

1. It's **sunny**.

2. It's **snowing**.

3. It's **hot**.

4. It's **cold**.

5. It's **windy**.

6. It's **raining**.

Listen and repeat.

B Listen.

Tien:	How's the weather?
Carlos:	It's **sunny**.

Listen and repeat.

C Look at Activity A. Talk with classmates about the pictures.

A: How's the weather?
B: It's _____.

How's the weather? 123

2 # It's hot!

 A Listen and circle.

1.

2.

3.

4.

B Complete.

windy   snowing   hot   ~~cold~~   raining   sunny

1. It's ___cold___ .   2. It's _____ .   3. It's _____ .

4. It's _____ .   5. It's _____ .   6. It's _____ .

3 What season do you like?

 A **Listen.**

1. winter   **2.** spring   **3.** summer   **4.** fall

Listen and repeat.

 B **Listen.**

Grace: What season do you like?
Leo: Winter.
Grace: What season don't you like?
Leo: Summer.

Listen and repeat.

Word List

winter
spring
summer
fall

C **Talk with 4 classmates.**

A: What season do you like?
B: _____.
A: What season don't you like?
B: _____.

MY LIFE **Talk in groups.**

What seasons do you like in your native country? What seasons don't you like in your native country? Why?

4 I'm dancing.

 A Listen.

1. walking   2. playing soccer   3. dancing   4. reading

5. swimming   6. listening to music   7. cooking   8. watching TV

Listen and repeat.

 B **Listen.**

Leo: What are you doing?
Nadira: I'm **walking**. What about you?
Leo: I'm **cooking**.

Listen and repeat.

C **Talk with 7 classmates.**

A: What are you doing?
B: I'm _____. What about you?
A: I'm _____.

Word List

playing soccer
watching TV
swimming
listening to music

5 What's Paul doing?

 A Listen and circle.

1.

2.

3.

4.

 B Listen.

Sandy:	What's **Justin** doing?
Will:	He's **playing basketball**.

Listen and repeat.

C Talk with 4 classmates.

A: What's _____ doing?
B: He's | _____.
    She's |

Word List

Grace/swimming
Leo/dancing
Ben/walking
Maria/talking

What do you like doing in the spring?

A **Listen.**

Isabel: What do you like doing in the **spring**?
Grace: I like **playing soccer**.
Isabel: What about in the **winter**?
Grace: I like **listening to music**.

Listen and repeat.

B **Talk to a partner.**

A: What do you like doing in the _____?
B: I like _____.
A: What about in the _____?
B: I like _____.

C **Ask 8 classmates.**

You: What do you like doing in the _____?

Name	Season	Activity
Carlos	spring	playing soccer
	summer	
	fall	
	winter	
	spring	
	summer	
	fall	
	winter	
	spring	

7 It's hot and dry.

 A **Listen and read.**

1. It's summer. It's **hot** and **dry**.

2. It's fall. It's **sunny** and **cool**.

3. It's winter. It's **cold** and **snowing**.

4. It's spring. It's **warm** and **windy**.

B **Write.**

1: In winter, it's _____ and _____.

2: In fall, it's _____ and _____.

3: In summer, it's _____ and _____.

4: In spring, it's _____ and _____.

MY LIFE   **Make a chart about the weather in your native country.**

I am from Russia.			
Season Weather		Season Weather	
Spring → warm and windy		Fall → cool	
Summer → hot and dry		Winter → cold and snowing	

Share your chart with your group.

8 What's the temperature?

Numbers

 A **Listen and write the numbers.**

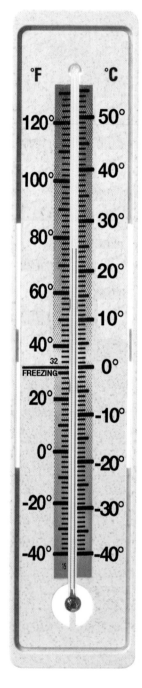

1. It's very hot.

   It's __105˚__ F. / It's _____ ° C.

   F = Fahrenheit
   C = Celsius

2. It's hot.

   It's _____ ° F. / It's _____ ° C.

3. It's warm.

   It's _____ ° F. / It's _____ ° C.

4. It's cool.

   It's _____ ° F. / It's _____ ° C.

5. It's cold.

   It's _____ ° F. / It's _____ ° C.

°F | **°C**

120° — 50°

100° — 40°

— 30°

80° — 20°

60° — 10°

40° —

32
FREEZING — 0°

20° — -10°

0° — -20°

-20° — -30°

-40° — -40°

9 A Weather Map

  A Listen and read the weather map.

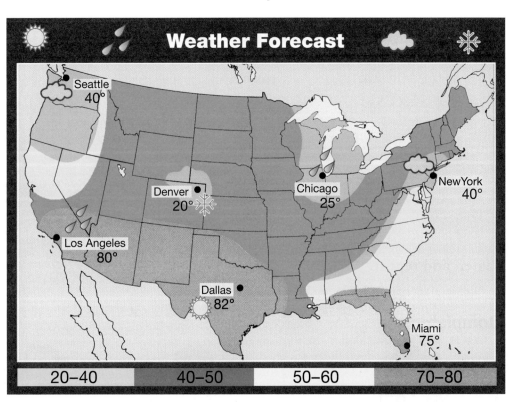

Weather Forecast

Seattle 40°

Denver 20°

Chicago 25°

New York 40°

Los Angeles 80°

Dallas 82°

Miami 75°

| 20–40 | 40–50 | 50–60 | 70–80 |

B Complete the chart.

City	Temperature	Sunny	Raining	Snowing	Cloudy
Seattle	40°				✔
Los Angeles					
Dallas					
Chicago					
Denver					
New York					
Miami					

C Write about the weather in your city.

The temperature is 25°F. The weather is sunny and cold.

Grammar: Present Continuous Tense

 A **Listen and read.**

PRESENT CONTINUOUS TENSE		
I	am	eating.
He	is	eating.
She	is	eating.
It	is	eating.
We	are	eating.
You	are	eating.
They	are	eating.

I'm eating a hamburger.

It's eating a hamburger, too.

Listen and repeat.

B **Complete.**

1. She _is_ read_ing_.

2. He ___ eat___.

3. They ___ listen___.

C **Write sentences.**

1. Tien/walk/to school _____ Tien is walking to school _____.

2. Sandy and I/play/soccer _____.

3. You and Nadira/watch/TV _____.

4. I/study/English _____.

132 Unit 8

Grammar: Contractions

 A **Listen and read.**

CONTRACTIONS		
I am studying.	→	**I'm** studying.
He is studying. **She is** studying. **It is** studying.	→ → →	**He's** studying. **She's** studying. **It's** studying.
We are studying. **You are** studying. **They are** studying.	→ → →	**We're** studying. **You're** studying. **They're** studying.

 B **Listen and complete.**

1. They__'re__ studying.   2. She_____ reading.   3. She_____ pointing.

C **Write about your classmates.**

Name		Activity
1. _____Leo_____	→	He's looking at the board.
2. _____	→	_____
3. _____	→	_____
4. _____	→	_____

Read: An Email

A **Listen and read.**

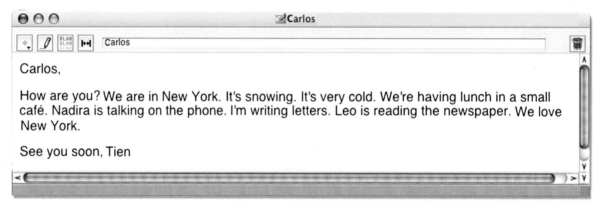

Carlos,

How are you? We are in New York. It's snowing. It's very cold. We're having lunch in a small café. Nadira is talking on the phone. I'm writing letters. Leo is reading the newspaper. We love New York.

See you soon, Tien

Read with a partner.

B **Complete. Add _–ing_.**

watch	drink	talk	snow	read	~~eat~~

1. Tien, Nadira, and Leo are _____eating_____ lunch.

2. It's very cold, and it's _____.

3. Leo is _____ the newspaper.

4. Tien is _____ coffee.

5. Nadira is _____ the snow and _____ on the phone.

13 Write: A Letter

 A **Listen and read.**

January 20, 2010

Dear Tien,

I'm in Miami. My family is here, too. It's winter. The weather here is sunny and very warm. Today we are swimming and having lunch at the beach. See you next week.

Your friend,
Carlos

Read with a partner.

B **Write a letter to a classmate.**

_____ , _____

Dear _____ ,

I'm in _____ . My _____ _____ here, too.

It's _____ . The weather here is _____ .

Today we are _____ .

See you next week.

_____ ,

_____

What do you know?

A Listen and write.

1. How's the ___weather___?

2. It's cold and _____.

3. My favorite season is _____.

4. I'm _____ soccer.

5. What are you _____?

6. They like _____ in the snow.

B Listen and fill in the answer sheet.

1. **A.** They're dancing.   **B.** They're swimming.

2. **A.** It's raining in New York.   **B.** It's snowing in New York.

3. **A.** What do you like doing   **B.** What's your favorite
       in the fall?   season?

4. **A.** It's a windy day.   **B.** It's a cloudy day.

5. **A.** Carlos is playing music.   **B.** Carlos is listening to music.

6. **A.** How's the weather?   **B.** What about you?

ANSWER SHEET		
1.	Ⓐ	Ⓑ
2.	Ⓐ	Ⓑ
3.	Ⓐ	Ⓑ
4.	Ⓐ	Ⓑ
5.	Ⓐ	Ⓑ
6.	Ⓐ	Ⓑ

C Listen and circle.

1. 16°F   60°F

2. windy   cloudy

3. 55°F   95°F

4. 14°F   40°F

5. cold   cloudy

6. snowing   sunny

D Write about you.

1. My favorite season is _____.

2. The weather is _____ and _____ today.

3. The temperature is _____ today.

4. **A:** What are you doing?

   B: I'm _____.

E **Ask 4 classmates.**

Leo: What do you like doing in the **winter**?
Tien: I like **watching TV**.
Leo: What about in the **spring**?
Tien: I like **walking**.

Name	Winter	Spring	Summer	Fall
Tien	watching TV	walking	swimming	reading

F ✔ **Check what you know.**

Learning Log

____ Celsius	____ hot	____ summer
____ cloudy	____ listen	____ sunny
____ cold	____ map	____ swim
____ cook	____ music	____ temperature
____ cool	____ play	____ walk
____ dance	____ raining	____ warm
____ degrees	____ read	____ watch
____ drink	____ season	____ weather
____ dry	____ snowing	____ weather map
____ Fahrenheit	____ soccer	____ windy
____ fall	____ spring	____ winter

LOOKING BACK Who do you see on page 122? Tell a partner.

Places Around Town

 A **Listen. Look at page 138.**

1. police station   2. bank   3. drugstore   4. hospital
5. fire station   6. gas station 7. library   8. post office

Listen and repeat.

 B **Listen.**

Maria: Where are you going?
Nadira: I'm going to the **post office**. What about you?
Maria: I'm going there, too. Let's go together.

Listen and repeat.

Word List

hospital
bank
drugstore
gas station
library

C **Talk with 6 classmates.**

A: Where are you going?
B: I'm going to the _____. What about you?
A: I'm going there, too. Let's go together.

D **Complete.**

| ~~drugstore~~ | fire station | hospital | post office |

1. ____drugstore____   2. _____

3. _____   4. _____

2 Neighborhood Map

A Write the places.

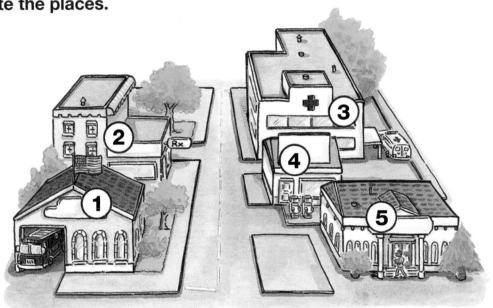

| fire station | library | hospital | drugstore | gas station |

1. _____fire station_____   2. _____

3. _____   4. _____

5. _____

B Listen.

Woman: Excuse me. Where's the **gas station**?
Grace: It's on **20th Street**.
Woman: On **20th Street**? Thanks.

Listen and repeat.

C Talk with 4 classmates.

A: Excuse me. Where's the _____?
B: It's on _____.
A: On _____? Thanks.

Word List

gas station/20th Street
hospital/19th Street
drugstore/South Avenue

3 More Places in the Neighborhood

 A Listen.

1. laundromat

2. movie theater

3. supermarket

4. bus stop

5. park

6. restaurant

Listen and repeat.

 B Listen.

Isabel:	Is there a **restaurant** in your neighborhood?
Leo:	**Yes, there is**.
Maria:	**No, there isn't**.

Listen and repeat.

C Talk with 7 classmates.

A: Is there a _____ in your neighborhood?
B: Yes, there is.
No, there isn't.

Word List

park
restaurant
movie theater
bus stop
laundromat
supermarket

4 Where's the bank?

 A **Listen and read.**

The restaurant is **on** Lake Avenue. It's **next to** the bank. The drugstore and the park are **on** 61st Street. The drugstore is **between** the park and the bank. The bank is **on** the corner. It's **on** the corner of 61st and Lake.

B **Listen.**

Ben: Where's the **bank**?
Paul: It's **on the corner**.
Ben: **On the corner**?
Paul: That's right. It's **between the drugstore and the restaurant**.

Listen and repeat.

C **Look at Activity A. Talk with 5 classmates.**

A: Where's the _____?
B: It's _____.
A: _____?
B: That's right. It's _____.

5 It's across from the bus stop.

 A **Listen.**

Carlos: Where's the **bus stop**?
Sandy: It's **across from** the **post office**.
Isabel: Where's the **laundromat**?
Sandy: It's **next to** the **park**.

Listen and repeat.

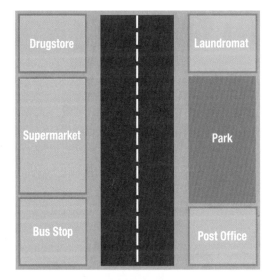

Drugstore
Laundromat
Supermarket
Park
Bus Stop
Post Office

B **Look at the map in Activity A. Talk with 4 classmates.**

A: Where's the _____?
B: It's _____ _____ the _____.

Word List

park
supermarket
drugstore
next to
across from

 C **Listen and write.**

1. The bus stop is _____next to_____ the supermarket.

2. The park is _____ the post office.

3. The drugstore is _____ from the laundromat.

4. The post office is _____ the bus stop.

5. The supermarket is _____ the drugstore and the bus stop.

MY LIFE **Make a map of important places in your neighborhood. Tell your group where they are.**

6 Do you live near a park?

A Listen.

1. He's **near** the bus stop.

2. They're **far from** the bus stop.

Listen and repeat.

B Listen and circle.

1. (near)   far from   2. near   far from

3. near   far from   4. near   far from

5. near   far from   6. near   far from

C Listen.

Sandy: Do you live **near a park**?
Tien: **Yes, I do.**
Paul: **No, I don't.**

Listen and repeat.

D Ask 5 classmates.

You: Do you live **far from a bus stop**?
Nadira: Yes, I do.
You: Please sign here.

far from a bus stop	near a park	near a drugstore
Nadira	_____	_____
far from a movie theater	near a bank	far from a supermarket
_____	_____	_____

7 Where do you buy stamps?

  A Listen.

1. see a movie   **2.** buy stamps   **3.** wash clothes   **4.** cash a check

Listen and repeat.

 B Listen.

Carlos: Where do you **buy stamps**?
Grace: At the **post office**.

Listen and repeat.

Word List

see a movie/movie theater
wash clothes/laundromat
cash a check/bank

C Talk with 4 classmates.

A: Where do you _____?
B: At the _____.

MY LIFE

Complete the sentences with things you do in your neighborhood.

I see movies at the _____movie theater_____.

I cash checks at the _____.

I wash clothes at the _____.

I _____ at the supermarket.

I _____ at school.

Read your sentences to your group.

8 A Deposit Slip

 A **Listen and read.**

Tien puts money in the bank every month. She is depositing money into her savings account. She is depositing a check. She is also depositing cash. This is her deposit slip.

DEPOSIT SLIP

Deposit TO THE ACCOUNT OF __Tien Lam__

ACCOUNT # __12-34565-43__   DATE __6/3/10__

DEPOSIT TO: *(PLEASE CHECK ONE)*

☐ Checking   ☒ Savings

1st **Cooperative Bank of Weston**

⑈012345⑈ ⑆123456543⑆01234567⑈

	Dollars	Cents
CASH	189	00
CHECKS 1.	42	95
2.		
3.		
TOTAL	231	95

B **Write the numbers.**

1. The date is _____June 3, 2010_____.

2. Tien's account number is _____.

3. She is depositing $ _____.

4. The check is for $ _____.

C **Circle.**

1. Tien is depositng money in her **checking/(savings)** account.

2. She's depositing **one check/two checks**.

3. Her cash deposit is **$189.00/$231.95**.

4. She is depositing a total of **$123.95/$231.95**.

5. June is the **fifth/sixth** month of the year.

9 Using an ATM

  A **Listen and read.**

Nadira is taking money from her checking account.
She's making a withdrawal from an ATM.
She is withdrawing $100.

> ATM = Automated Teller Machine
>
> PIN = Personal Identification Number

1. Put your ATM card in the slot.

Enter PIN / xxxx

2. Type your PIN. Then push *Enter*.

Withdrawal
Deposit
Check balance

3. Pick what you want to do.

Amount
$20
$50
$100
$200

4. Pick the amount. Take the money.

B **Look at Activity A. Circle.**

1. Nadira inserts her ATM _____. check (card)

2. Her PIN is 2679. She presses _____. 2-6-7-9 9-7-6-2

3. She is making a _____. withdrawal deposit

4. She is taking out _____. $100 $200

Grammar: Prepositions of Place

 A Listen and read.

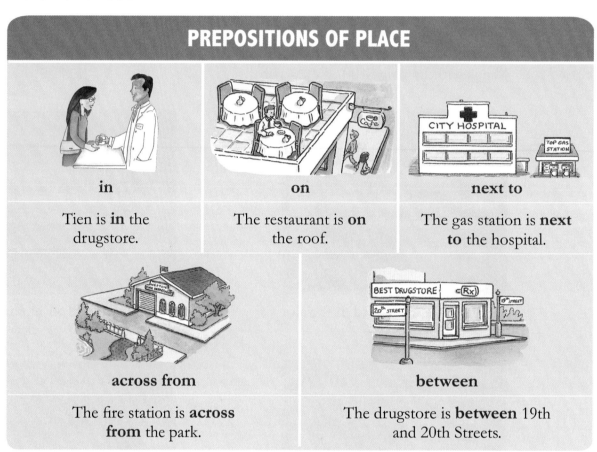

PREPOSITIONS OF PLACE

in

Tien is **in** the drugstore.

on

The restaurant is **on** the roof.

next to

The gas station is **next to** the hospital.

across from

The fire station is **across from** the park.

between

The drugstore is **between** 19th and 20th Streets.

Listen and repeat.

 B Listen and ✔ check.

	in	on	next to	across from	between
1.		✔			
2.					
3.					
4.					
5.					
6.					

Grammar: Preposition Practice

A Write *in* or *on*.

1. Paul is working ___on___ the computer.

2. He is _____ the library.

3. His book is _____ the table.

4. Paul lives _____ Los Angeles.

5. He lives _____ School Street.

6. Paul's computer is _____ the table.

B Write *next to*, *between*, or *across from*.

1. The drugstore is ___next to___ the supermarket.

2. The park is _____ the post office and the laundromat.

3. The park is _____ the laundromat.

4. The bus stop is _____ the post office.

5. The supermarket is _____ the bus stop and the drugstore.

6. The post office is _____ the park.

7. The laundromat is _____ the drugstore.

8. The supermarket is _____ the park.

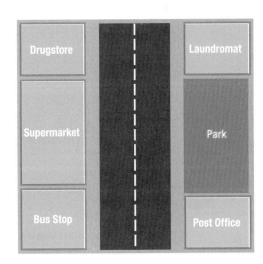

Read: Cashing a Check

  A **Listen and read.**

Cashing a Check

Ben gets his paycheck on Friday. His check is $154.85. He has a savings account at the bank. Usually he brings his check there. The teller gives Ben $154.85.

Today is Saturday. The bank is closed. So Ben goes to a check cashing store. The clerk takes Ben's check. She gives him $144.85. She keeps $10. It costs $10 at the check cashing store. Ben is angry. He needs all the money.

Read with a partner.

B ✔ **Check.**

What is the story about?

_____ **1.** Ben cashes a check.   _____ **2.** Ben goes to the bank.

C **Look at Activity A. Complete.**

1. The bank is closed on _____Saturday_____.

2. Ben's paycheck is $ _____.

3. Ben gets $ _____ at the bank.

4. Ben gets $ _____ at the check cashing store.

5. Ben doesn't pay to cash his check at the _____.

6. Ben pays $10.00 to cash his check at the _____.

13 Write: An Application

A Read.

Carlos is at the supermarket. He wants to pay by check. He needs a special card. He completes this form.

SUNNY SUPERMARKET **Card Club** Application

AVILA	CARLOS	818-555-0012
Last Name	First Name	Home Phone

18921 17TH AVENUE		6 P
Street Address		Apartment #

LOS ANGELES	CA	90021-0301	030688
City	State	Zip Code	Date of Birth (month/day/year)

K98098-K48	► *Carlos Avila* 10/14/2010	
Driver's License Number or State I.D. Number	Applicant's Signature Date	

. . . .

B Complete for you.

SUNNY SUPERMARKET **Card Club** Application

		- -
Last Name	First Name	Home Phone

Street Address		Apartment #

		-	
City	State	Zip Code	Date of Birth (month/day/year)

-	►	
Driver's License Number or State I.D. Number	Applicant's Signature Date	

What do you know?

 A **Listen and write.**

1. **Sandy:** Do you live _____far from_____ a bus stop?

   Tien: No, I _____.

   Sandy: Do you live _____ a park?

   Tien: _____, I do.

2. **Isabel:** _____ me. Where is the police station?

   Leo: It's _____ 54th Street, _____

   _____ the park.

   Isabel: _____.

 B **Listen and fill in the answer sheet.**

1. **A.** police station   **B.** hospital

2. **A.** bus stop   **B.** fire station

3. **A.** next to   **B.** across from

4. **A.** movie theater   **B.** restaurant

5. **A.** wash clothes   **B.** buy stamps

6. **A.** ATM   **B.** deposit

ANSWER SHEET

1. (A) (●B)
2. (A) (B)
3. (A) (B)
4. (A) (B)
5. (A) (B)
6. (A) (B)

 C **Listen and fill in the answer sheet.**

1. They're in the ____. **A.** laundromat   **B.** restaurant

2. They're in the ____. **A.** movie theater   **B.** fire station

3. They're in the ____. **A.** supermarket   **B.** bank

4. They're in the ____. **A.** post office   **B.** drugstore

5. They're in the ____. **A.** laundromat   **B.** gas station

6. They're in the ____. **A.** library   **B.** supermarket

ANSWER SHEET

1. (A) (●B)
2. (A) (B)
3. (A) (B)
4. (A) (B)
5. (A) (B)
6. (A) (B)

1. I live on _____.
   (Street/Avenue/Road)

2. My address is _____.

3. My house is near a _____.

E **Complete.**

| from | gas | neighborhood | ~~on~~ | washes |

Leo lives in an apartment building. It is ___on___ Water Street. His building is near a _____ station. Leo lives across _____ a laundromat. He _____ his clothes there. Leo likes his _____.

F ✔ **Check what you know.**

Learning Log

____ account number	____ drugstore	____ next to
____ across from	____ excuse me	____ on
____ application	____ far from	____ park
____ ATM	____ fire station	____ PIN
____ bank	____ gas station	____ police station
____ between	____ hospital	____ post office
____ bus stop	____ in	____ restaurant
____ buy stamps	____ laundromat	____ savings account
____ cash a check	____ library	____ see a movie
____ checking account	____ make a deposit	____ supermarket
____ corner	____ movie theater	____ thanks
____ deposit	____ near	____ wash clothes
____ deposit slip	____ neighborhood	____ withdrawal

LOOKING BACK Look at page 138. What do you see? Tell a partner.

Review for Units 7–9

CONTRACTIONS WITH *BE*

I**'m** from Mexico.

He**'s** from Mexico.
She**'s** from Mexico.
It**'s** from Mexico.

We**'re** from Mexico.
You**'re** from Mexico.
They**'re** from Mexico.

A **Write the contractions:
'm, 's, or 're.**

1. I**'m** from Mexico.

2. You____ from Haiti.

3. They____ from the USA.

4. She____ from China.

5. We____ from Russia.

6. I____ from _____.

PRESENT CONTINUOUS TENSE

I **am** work**ing**. He **is** work**ing**. She **is** work**ing**. It **is** work**ing**.	We **are** work**ing**. You **are** work**ing**. They **are** work**ing**.

B **Complete. Use the present continuous tense.**

1. Carlos is in the park. _____He is walking_____ with his dog.
   He/walk

2. Ben and Grace are in a restaurant. _____ lunch.
   They/eat

3. Tien is in the bank. _____ money.
   She/withdraw

4. You and Leo are in the library. _____ books.
   You/read

5. I'm in the post office. _____ stamps.
   I/buy

6. You and I are at a laundromat. _____ our clothes.
   We/wash

C Talk in groups.

What are you doing now?

D Listen and circle.

1.

It's windy.

(It's raining.)

2.

They're dancing.

They're playing soccer.

3.

It's cloudy.

It's sunny.

4.

She's swimming.

She's walking.

E Complete.

| aisle 3 | ~~carton~~ | jar | laundromat | bank | milk | summer |

1. I need a _____ carton _____ of orange juice.
2. I have a _____ of peanut butter.
3. Bread is in _____.
4. I wash my clothes at the _____.
5. I usually drink _____ for breakfast.
6. I like swimming in the _____.
7. I deposit money at the _____.

A Circle the types of marketplaces. <u>Underline</u> the countries.

A (farm stand) in the <u>US</u>

A street market in Grenada

A fish market in Japan

A floating market in Thailand

A night market in Taiwan   A supermarket in Canada

B Think about it. Complete the chart. Where do you get food?

Food	In my native country	in the USA
fish	at a fish market	
dairy		
bread		
fruit		
meat		
vegetables		

C Talk in groups.

In my country we buy fish at the fish market. In the US, I buy fish at a supermarket.

157

You need to see a doctor.

Where are the people?
What do you see?

1 What's the matter?

  A **Listen.**

1. an earache

2. a sore throat

3. a headache

4. a broken arm

5. a toothache

6. a stomachache

7. a backache

8. a cold

Listen and repeat.

 B **Listen.**

Nurse: What's the matter?
Maria: I have **a headache**.

Listen and repeat.

C **Talk with 6 classmates.**

A: What's the matter?
B: I have a _____.

Word List

backache
cold
headache
stomachache
toothache

2 His hand hurts.

 A **Listen.**

1. head
2. eye
3. nose
4. chest
5. stomach
6. leg
7. foot
8. finger
9. hand
10. arm

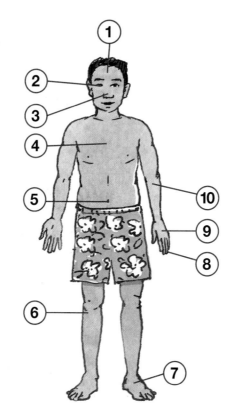

Listen and repeat.

 B **Listen.**

Sandy: What's the matter with **Ben**?
Leo: His **hand** hurts.

Listen and repeat.

C **Talk with a partner.**

A: What's the matter with _____?
B: His | _____ hurts.
     Her |

Word List

Tien/ear
Paul/arm
Leo/finger
Maria/head
Nadira/stomach

A **Listen.**

Ana: I feel bad. My **ear** hurts.
Maria: You need to see a doctor.

Listen and repeat.

B **Talk with a partner.**

A: I feel bad. My _____ hurts.
B: You need to see a doctor.

Word List

eye
chest
hand
leg
foot
finger

C **Listen.**

Maria: Hello. This is **Maria Cruz**. My
daughter is sick. Can Dr. Brown see
her today?
Man: Yes. Dr. Brown can see **her** at **10:00**.
Maria: Today at **10:00**? That's fine.
Thank you.

Listen and repeat.

MY LIFE   **Write a phone conversation about a relative.**

A: Hello. This is _____. My _____ is sick.

Can Dr. Brown see _____ today?

B: Yes. Dr. Brown can see _____ at

_____.

A: Today at _____? That's fine. Thank you.

Practice with a partner.

Health Problems and Remedies

  **A** **Listen to the health problems.**

 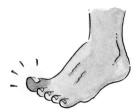 

1. a cut   **2.** a cough   **3.** an infection   **4.** a fever

Listen and repeat.

 B **Listen to the health remedies.**

  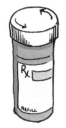 

1. a bandage   **2.** cough syrup   **3.** an antibiotic   **4.** aspirin

Listen and repeat.

 C **Listen and ✔ check.**

	1. Isabel	2. Carlos	3. Don	4. Leo	5. Nadira
a cut	✔				
a fever					
an infection					
a cough					
an antibiotic					
aspirin					
a bandage	✔				
cough syrup					

5 She needs a bandage.

 A **Listen.**

Ben: Lin has **a cut on her arm**.
Grace: That's too bad. She needs **a bandage**.

Listen and repeat.

B **Talk with 5 classmates.**

A: Leo has _____.
B: That's too bad. He needs _____.

Word List

a cough/cough syrup
a headache/aspirin
a cut/a bandage
an infection/an antibiotic

 C **Listen. Complete the chart.**

Name	Health Problem	Body Part	Health Remedy
1. Leo	cough	throat	cough syrup
2. Isabel			
3. Carlos			
4. Nadira			

6 I exercise.

 A **Listen.**

1. exercise

2. drink water

3. don't smoke

4. get enough sleep

5. eat healthy food

6. don't eat junk food

Listen and repeat.

B ✔ **Check what you do.**

____ I exercise.　　　　____ I get enough sleep.　　　　____ I don't eat junk food.

____ I drink water.　　　____ I eat healthy food.　　　　____ I don't smoke.

C **Look at your answers in Activity B. Talk with 7 classmates.**

A: I _____.
B: I don't _____.

I get enough sleep.　　I don't smoke.

7 Home Remedies

 A Listen.

1. Drink hot water. **2.** Take a hot shower. **3.** Drink orange juice. **4.** Rest.

Listen and repeat.

 B Listen.

Paul: I have a **cough**.
Isabel: **Take a hot shower.**
Leo: **Drink hot water.**

C Talk with 4 classmates.

A: I have a _____.
B: _____.

Word List

sore throat/take a hot shower
stomachache/drink hot water
cold/drink orange juice

MY LIFE **Write home remedies for these health problems.**

cough: _____Drink hot water with lemon_____.

cough: _____.

cold: _____.

fever: _____.

cut: _____.

Read your sentences in groups.

Taking Medicine

  **A** **Listen.**

 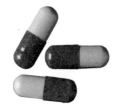  

1. pills **2.** capsules **3.** a teaspoon of medicine **4.** drops

Listen and repeat.

 B **Listen.**

| 1x | 2x | 3x |

1. once **2.** twice **3.** three times

Listen and repeat.

C **Circle the answers in the chart.**

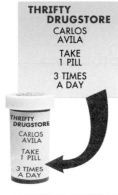  

Carlos	a pill	a capsule	drops	1x	2x	3x
Leo	a pill	a capsule	drops	1x	2x	3x
Isabel	a pill	a capsule	drops	1x	2x	3x

(Carlos row: "a pill" is circled)

Health Insurance

 A **Listen and read.**

Grace has a health insurance card. She needs the card to see a doctor. Her health insurance is from Ben's work.

Community Health Care Group   POS

Name of Insured: **Grace Lee**   ID#: **90933MC**

D.O.B.: **3/16/1980**

Name of Employee: **Ben Lee**   Plan: **Family**

Co-payment: **$15.00**   *Grace Lee*

Co-payment =
Money you
pay to see a
doctor

D.O.B. =
Date Of Birth

B **Complete the form for Grace.**

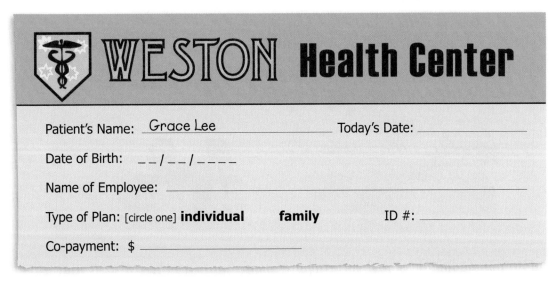

WESTON Health Center

Patient's Name: _Grace Lee_____   Today's Date: _____

Date of Birth: __ / __ / ____

Name of Employee: _____

Type of Plan: [circle one] **individual**   **family**   ID #: _____

Co-payment: $ _____

Grammar: Action Verbs

  A **Listen and read.**

ACTION VERBS	
I run.	**He** runs.
You run.	**She** runs.
We run.	**It** runs.
They run.	

I run every day.

Listen and repeat.

B **Look at the picture. Write the verbs in the correct form.**

lift weights	play soccer	run	swim	walk

1. Ben and Paul _____ run _____.　　2. Leo _____.

3. Nadira and Grace _____.　　4. Isabel _____.

5. Carlos _____.　　6. The dog _____.

11 Grammar: Negatives

 A **Listen and read.**

I don't swim.

NEGATIVES	
I **don't** swim.	He **doesn't** swim.
You **don't** swim.	She **doesn't** swim.
We **don't** swim.	It **doesn't** swim.
They **don't** swim.	

Listen and repeat.

 B **Listen and write the number.**

a. _____

b. _____

c. _____

d. _____

C **Complete. Write the negative.**

1. I eat fruit. He _____doesn't_____ _____eat_____ fruit.

2. We swim. She _____ _____.

3. He lifts weights. I _____ _____ weights.

4. They dance. We _____ _____.

You need to see a doctor. 169

 A **Listen and read.**

The Goldman Sisters

Frances and Eleanor Goldman are sisters. They are healthy. Eleanor is 81 years old. Frances is 83. They exercise and eat healthy food every day. Frances likes apples. Eleanor likes oranges. They drink water. They get enough sleep. They don't smoke.

Eleanor likes to walk her white dog. Frances likes to walk, too. She has a big dog. Frances says, "Be healthy. Get a dog." Eleanor says, "Be healthy. Don't eat junk food."

Read with a partner.

B **Complete.**

likes apples	~~healthy~~	~~81~~	
exercise	walk a lot	83	has a large dog
drink water	likes oranges	don't smoke	has a white dog

Eleanor   Eleanor and Frances   Frances

81

healthy

13 Write: A Health Plan

  A Listen and read Tien's health plan.

Dr. Jones has a plan for Tien.

1. Walk every day.
2. Exercise.
3. Drink a lot of water.
4. Don't eat junk food.
5. Don't smoke.

B Write your health plan.

My health plan

1. _____Get enough sleep._____
2. _____
3. _____
4. _____
5. _____
6. _____

Word List

walk
drink water
eat healthy food
exercise
smoke
sleep

Read your health plan to your group.

What do you know?

A Write.

| a toothache | a headache | a cut |
| a sore throat | a stomachache | a cold |

1. <u>a toothache</u>

2. _____

3. _____

4. _____

5. _____

6. _____

B Listen and fill in the answer sheet.

1. **A.** I have a headache. **B.** I have an infection.

2. **A.** Yes. Dr. Wall can see you at 2:00. **B.** Yes, Dr. Wall can see you at 3:00.

3. **A.** Drink hot water. **B.** Take a hot shower.

4. **A.** Her ear hurts. **B.** Her throat hurts.

5. **A.** Yes. I exercise and don't smoke. **B.** Yes. I exercise and walk every day.

ANSWER SHEET

1. (A) (B)
2. (A) (B)
3. (A) (B)
4. (A) (B)
5. (A) (B)

C Write.

Doctor: What's the matter?

You: I have a _____.

Doctor: That's too bad. You need _____.

D **Read each health problem. Write a remedy.**

1. I have a headache. _____Take some aspirin._____ .

2. I have a cough. _____ .

3. I have a stomachache. _____ .

4. I have a cold. _____ .

5. I have a fever. _____ .

E ✔ **Check what you know.**

Learning Log

____ antibiotic	____ eye	____ pill
____ arm	____ fever	____ raise
____ aspirin	____ finger	____ rest
____ backache	____ foot	____ run
____ bandage	____ hand	____ sick
____ broken arm	____ head	____ sleep
____ capsule	____ headache	____ smoke
____ chest	____ health insurance	____ sore throat
____ cold	____ healthy	____ stomach
____ co-payment	____ home remedy	____ stomachache
____ cough	____ hurt	____ stretch
____ cough syrup	____ infection	____ swim
____ cut	____ junk food	____ teaspoon
____ drink	____ leg	____ three times
____ drops	____ lift weights	____ toes
____ ear	____ medicine	____ toothache
____ earache	____ nose	____ touch
____ enough	____ once	____ twice
____ exercise	____ orange juice	____ water

🔍 **LOOKING BACK Look at page 158. What do you see? Tell a partner.**

What jobs do you see?

1 What do you do?

A Listen. Look at page 174.

1. a sales clerk
2. a taxi driver
3. a health aide
4. a waiter
5. a cook
6. a cashier
7. a construction worker
8. a delivery person
9. an office worker
10. a computer programmer

Listen and repeat.

B Listen.

Carlos: What do you do?
Maria: I'm **a sales clerk**. And you?
Carlos: I'm **a waiter**.

Listen and repeat.

C Talk with a partner.

A: What do you do?
B: I'm _____. And you?
A: I'm _____.

D Look at the picture on page 174. Complete.

1. Ben is ____a construction worker____.
2. Leo is _____.
3. Nadira is _____.
4. Isabel is _____.
5. Paul is _____.
6. Tien is _____.

A cook uses pots and pans.

 A Listen.

1. a taxicab

2. an order pad

3. pots and pans

4. a computer

5. a cash register

6. tools

Listen and repeat.

B Match.

_e_ **1.** cashier   **a.** taxicab

____ **2.** construction worker   **b.** an order pad

____ **3.** cook   **c.** pots and pans

____ **4.** office worker   **d.** a computer

____ **5.** taxi driver   e. a cash register

____ **6.** waiter   **f.** tools

 C Listen and circle.

1. (office worker)   taxi driver   **2.** construction worker   cook

3. waiter   taxi driver   **4.** office worker   cashier

5. taxi driver   cook   **6.** construction worker   waiter

3 Do you like to work outdoors?

 A **Listen.**

   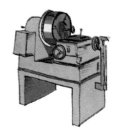

1. indoors   2. outdoors   3. with people   4. with machines

Listen and repeat.

B ✔ **Check.**

Jobs	Indoors	Outdoors	With People	With Machines
construction worker		✔		✔
waiter				
sales clerk				
delivery person				

 C **Listen.**

Grace: Do you like to work **outdoors**?
Tien: **Yes, I do.** And you?
Grace: **No, I don't.**

Listen and repeat.

Word List

indoors
outdoors
with machines
with people

D **Talk with 5 classmates.**

A: Do you like to work _____?
B: │Yes, I do.
    │No, I don't.

What's your job? 177

4 I can use a computer.

 A **Listen.**

1. drive

2. fix

3. sell

4. cook

5. use

6. deliver

Listen and repeat.

 B **Listen.**

Leo: What can you do?
Paul: I can **use a computer**. And you?
Leo: I can **drive a car**.

Listen and repeat.

I can use a
computer.

C **Talk with 6 classmates.**

A: What can you do?
B: I can _____. And you?
A: I can _____.

MY LIFE **Talk about your job.**

What is your job? What do you use at your job?

Tell your group.

Yes, I can.

 A **Listen.**

Man:	Can you **sell clothes**?
Maria:	**Yes, I can.**
Man:	Can you **use tools**?
Maria:	**No, I can't.**

Listen and repeat.

B **Talk with 6 classmates.**

A: Can you _____?
B: Yes, I can.
No, I can't.

Word List

deliver boxes
fix things
help people
cook meals
use a computer

C **Write about you.**

1. I can _____

   _____.

2. I can _____

   _____.

3. I can't _____

   _____.

4. I can't _____

   _____.

Read your sentences to a partner.

I can fix a house. I can't speak Spanish.

6 Reading Want Ads

A Read the want ads. Circle the jobs.

1.

Allman Shop at Low Creek Mall. Seeking 2 (cashiers.) Call Mr. Howard (781) 555-6789.

2.

Waiter Needed Days
No experience.
Kim's Family Restaurant
El Paso, Texas
See Wendy.

3.

Help Needed
Health aide in my home
Tues.-Fri. 5:00-9:00 p.m.
Mrs. Flores
(312) 555-1144

B Match.

1. __C__ Who do you speak to at Kim's Family Restaurant?
2. ____ Who needs a health aide?
3. ____ What is the phone number at the Allman Shop?
4. ____ When is the health aide needed?
5. ____ Where is Kim's Family Restaurant?
6. ____ What jobs are open at the Allman Shop?

a. cashiers
b. El Paso
c. Wendy
d. Mrs. Flores
e. (781) 555-6789
f. 5:00-9:00 P.M.

C Listen and ✔ check the ad from Activity A.

Names	Ad #1	Ad #2	Ad #3
1. Lina	✔		
2. Carlos			
3. Pavel			
4. Nadira			
5. Betty			
6. Pablo			

7   I was a cashier.

 A   **Listen.**

Sandy:	What did you do before?
Maria:	I was a **cashier** in **Mexico**.
Grace and Ben:	We were **students** in **China**.

Grace and Ben before

Maria before

Listen and repeat.

B   **Talk with a partner.**

A: What did you do before?

B: I was   a   _____ in _____.
        an   (work)   (country)

C   **Complete the chart. Ask 7 classmates.**

Name	Work	Country
Maria	cashier	Mexico

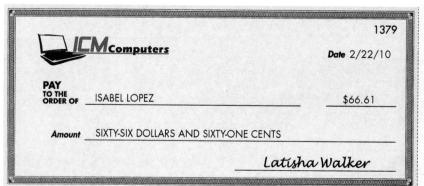

ICM Computers	1379	ISABEL LOPEZ	1379
	Date 2/22/10	Pay Rate:	$10.00/hour
		Hours:	8
PAY TO THE ORDER OF ISABEL LOPEZ	$66.61	Gross Pay:	$80.00

DEDUCTIONS
Federal Tax: 7.09
State Tax: 2.95
FICA: 1.58
Medicare: 1.77
Total Deductions $13.39

Amount SIXTY-SIX DOLLARS AND SIXTY-ONE CENTS

Latisha Walker

 A Listen and read.

Isabel is an office worker. She works at ICM computers. Isabel makes $10 an hour. She usually works eight hours a week. She makes $80 a week.

Isabel has to pay taxes. She pays $7.09 in federal taxes. She pays $2.95 in state taxes. Isabel pays other taxes, too. Her paycheck is $66.61. That is her take-home pay.

Read with a partner.

B Circle.

1. The paycheck is for ____.   (Isabel Lopez)   Latisha Walker

2. Isabel makes ____. $8 an hour $10 an hour

3. Isabel works ____.   8 hours a week   10 hours a week

4. Isabel's federal taxes are ____. $2.95 $7.09

5. Isabel's state taxes are ____. $2.95 $7.09

6. Isabel's take-home pay is ____. $66.61 $80.00

C Write.

1. Isabel works 10 hours a week. Her gross pay is $ _____.

2. Isabel's total deductions are $13.39. Her take-home pay is $ _____.

  A Listen and read.

a. Caution Work Area

b. Fire Extinguisher

c. High Voltage
KEEP OUT

d. No Smoking

e. Emergency Exit

f. Wash Hands

B Look at Activity A. Match.

_c_ **1.** Don't go inside.

___ **2.** Use this door in an emergency.

___ **3.** Don't smoke.

___ **4.** Be careful.

___ **5.** Use soap and water.

___ **6.** Use to put out a fire.

C Make a safety sign for work or school. Tell a partner.

Don't eat food in class.

Grammar: Simple Past of *Be*

 A **Listen and read.**

SIMPLE PAST OF *BE*	
Singular	**Plural**
I **was** a student.	We **were** students.
You **were** a student.	You **were** students.
He **was** a student. She **was** a student.	They **were** students.

Sandy **was** a student in 1978.

Listen and repeat.

 B **Listen and circle.**

1. (present)   past   2. present   past

3. present   past   4. present   past

5. present   past   6. present   past

Words about the past

Yesterday
Last (week/month/year)
(Two days/Many years) **ago**
in (August/1990)

 C **Complete. Write *was* or *were*.**

1. Nadira _____ was _____ a cook in Somalia two years ago.

2. In 2004 you _____ an office worker.

3. Yesterday my son Nestor _____ sick.

4. Paul and I _____ students in 2006.

5. In January, my sisters _____ in Texas.

6. Last year, I _____ a waiter in Brazil.

D **Write about you.**

In 2000 I _____. In 2004 my family and I _____.

Grammar: *Can/Can't*

CAN/CAN'T		
Questions	Yes	No
Can you **drive** a car?	Yes, I can.	No, I can't.
Can he **use** a computer?	Yes, he can.	No, he can't.

A Write *can* or *can't*.

1. Paul is a computer programmer. He _____can_____ use a computer.

2. Tien speaks English and Vietnamese. She _____ speak Portuguese.

3. Ben is a construction worker. He _____ use tools.

4. Leo is a taxi driver. He _____ drive a car.

5. The bank is closed. Isabel _____ deposit her paycheck.

6. Maria needs to be home at 3:00 P.M. She _____ work in the afternoon.

B Ask 8 classmates.

You: Can you **drive a car**?
Isabel: **Yes, I can.**
You: Please sign here.

sell clothes	cook a meal	fix a house
_____	_____	_____
use a cash register	drive a car Isabel	deliver boxes
_____	_____	_____
use tools	use a computer	work with machines
_____	_____	_____

12 Read: A Job Application

A **Read.**

Leo wants a new job. He goes to Hilltop Company. He completes a job application.

Hilltop COMPANY

Human Resources
JOB APPLICATION

PERSONAL INFORMATION

Name	Leonid Danovinski **PAST**	Leo Danov **PRESENT**
Address	Novy Arbat Street, Moscow, Russia	17 Water Street, Los Angeles, CA 90001
Telephone	—	312-555-6533

EDUCATION

School	Moscow Secondary School	ESL class, City College

EMPLOYMENT

JOB	EMPLOYER	DATES
Taxi Driver	Swift Taxi, Inc.	2003–present
Delivery Person	On-Time Delivery Co.	1999–2003

SKILLS (CHECK WHAT YOU CAN DO.)

☐ Type   ☐ Cook   ☐ Use a computer   ☐ Fix machines   Drive: ☒ car   ☒ van   ☐ truck

☐ Languages _Russian, Polish, Slovak, and English_

Signature _Leo Danov_   Date _February 15, 2010_

B **Write the answers.**

1. Where does Leo live? ___17 Water Street, Los Angeles, CA___

2. Where did Leo go to school? _____

3. What is Leo's job? _____

4. What was Leo's job before? _____

5. Can Leo drive a truck? _____

6. Can Leo speak Slovak? _____

186 Unit 11

13 Write: A Telephone Conversation

 A Listen and read.

Maria wants a new job, too. She is calling Mr. Brand at City Hospital.

Maria:	Good morning, Mr. Brand. I'm calling about the job in the hospital gift shop. I work at Best Department Store now. I sell watches.
Mr. Brand:	What did you do before?
Maria:	I was a cashier in Mexico. I can use a cash register.
Mr. Brand:	Can you speak Spanish and Portuguese?
Maria:	I can speak Spanish and English. I can't speak Portuguese.
Mr. Brand:	When can you work?
Maria:	I can work Monday to Friday from 8:00 A.M. to 3:00 P.M.
Mr. Brand:	There is an opening from 8:00 A.M. to noon Monday to Thursday. Is that good for you?
Maria:	Yes, it is. Thank you.

Read with a partner.

B Write a conversation for a job you want.

You: Good morning, Mr. Brand. I'm calling about _____
_____
_____

Mr. Brand: What did you do before?

You: _____

Mr. Brand: Can you _____

You: I can _____

I can't _____

Mr. Brand: When can you work?

You: _____

Mr. Brand: There is an opening _____

Is that good for you?

You: Yes, it is. Thank you.

Practice with a partner.

What's your job? 187

What do you know?

A Write the job.

cashier	cook	~~delivery person~~
office worker	taxi driver	waiter

1. <u>delivery person</u>   2. _____   3. _____

4. _____   5. _____   6. _____

B Listen and fill in the answer sheet.

1. **A.** construction worker   **B.** computer programmer
2. **A.** order pad   **B.** tools
3. **A.** What is your job?   **B.** What did you do before?
4. **A.** I'm a health aide.   **B.** I was a health aide.
5. **A.** Yes, I can.   **B.** No, I can't.

ANSWER SHEET

1. (A) (B)
2. (A) (B)
3. (A) (B)
4. (A) (B)
5. (A) (B)

C Find a want ad. Look in a newspaper or online. Complete.

1. Job: _____

2. Address: _____

3. Phone number: _____

D Complete the form.

C.L.T. Human Resources	Job Application

LAST NAME _____ FIRST NAME _____ MI ____

ADDRESS _____ CITY _____ STATE _____ ZIP CODE _____

Telephone Number: (_ _ _) _ _ _ - _ _ _ _

LAST JOB: _____ DATES: _____

EMPLOYER: _____

E ✔ Check what you know.

Learning Log

—— application
—— cash register
—— cashier
—— caution
—— computer
—— computer programmer
—— construction worker
—— cook
—— deliver
—— delivery person
—— drive
—— emergency
—— employer
—— exit

—— fire extinguisher
—— fix
—— health aide
—— high voltage
—— indoors
—— job application
—— keep out
—— machines
—— office worker
—— order pad
—— outdoors
—— paycheck
—— people
—— pots and pans

—— safety signs
—— sales clerk
—— sell
—— take-home pay
—— taxes
—— taxi cab
—— taxi driver
—— tools
—— use
—— waiter
—— want ad
—— was
—— were
—— work

LOOKING BACK Look at page 174. What do you see? Tell a partner.

How do you get to school?

What do you see?

1 I take a bus.

 A **Listen.**

1. take a bus

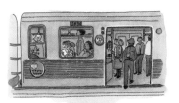

2. take a subway

3. ride a bike

4. drive a car

5. walk

6. take a taxi

Listen and repeat.

B **Ask 8 classmates.**

You: How do you get to school?
Leo: I **take a taxi**.
You: Please sign here.

walk	take a subway	take a taxi
_____	_____	_Leo_____
take a bus	drive a car	ride a bike
_____	_____	_____
walk	take a bus	drive a car
_____	_____	_____

2 It's on the left.

 A **Listen.**

←
1. on the left

↑
2. straight ahead

→
3. on the right

Listen and repeat.

 B **Listen.**

Maria: Excuse me. Where is the **movie theater**?
Man: It's **on the left**.

Listen and repeat.

C **Look at the picture in Activity A. Talk with 3 classmates.**

A: Excuse me. Where is the _____?
B: It's _____.

 D **Listen and circle.**

1. on the left   straight ahead   (on the right)

2. on the left   straight ahead   on the right

3. on the left   straight ahead   on the right

4. on the left   straight ahead   on the right

3 It's next to the market.

 **A** Listen.

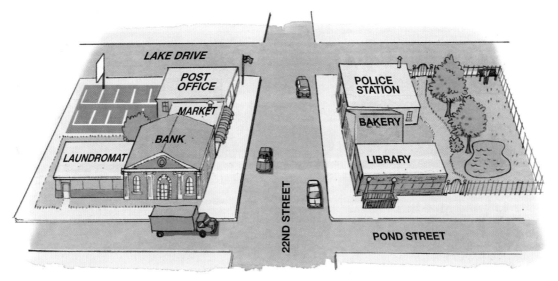

1. on the corner of
4. behind

2. next to
5. across from

3. between
6. near

Listen and repeat.

- -

 B Listen.

Maria: Excuse me. Where is **the post office**?

Man: It's **next to the market**.

Listen and repeat.

- -

C Look at the picture in Activity A. Talk with 5 classmates.

A: Excuse me. Where is the _____?

B: It's _____.

How do I get to the airport?

 **A** **Match.**

M-4 TO WESTSIDE PARK   108 TO BROOKLINE   D TRAIN TO DOWNTOWN CIRCLE   RED LINE- MIDWAY AIRPORT

1. __c__ M-4 Bus   **a.** Midway Airport

2. ____ 108 Bus   **b.** Downtown Circle

3. ____ D Train   **c.** Westside Park

4. ____ Red Line   **d.** Brookline

 B **Listen.**

Paul: How do I get to **Midway Airport**?
Sandy: Take the **Red Line**.
Paul: The **Red Line**? Thanks.

Listen and repeat.

C **Talk with 6 classmates.**

A: How do I get to _____?
B: Take the _____.
A: The _____? Thanks.

5 When does the next train leave?

 A **Listen.**

Carlos: When does the next train to **Miami** leave?
Woman: It leaves at **4:20**.
Carlos: At **4:20**? Thanks.

Listen and repeat.

B **Talk to 4 classmates.**

A: When does the next train to _____ leave?
B: It leaves at _____.
A: At _____? Thanks.

Word List

Miami/4:20
New York/1:30
Seattle/8:45
Dallas/12:00

 C **Listen and circle.**

Where?	When?
1. Cincinnati / (Chicago)	(6:14) / 6:40
2. Oakland / Los Angeles	9:00 / 10:00
3. Tempe / Tucson	2:00 / 12:00
4. Newtown / Newark	10:02 / 10:12
5. Boston / New York	8:30 / 12:00
6. Miami / Orlando	5:15 / 5:50
7. San Antonio / Santa Fe	2:13 / 2:30
8. San Diego / Riverside	3:11 / 11:03

6 Getting a Learner's Permit

 A **Listen and read.**

Nadira wants to drive to school. She needs a learner's permit. She finished the driver's education class last week. Now she needs to take a test to get a learner's permit. She calls to make an appointment. She can take the test on Thursday. The test costs $26. Leo can teach Nadira to drive after the test.

Read with a partner.

B **Circle.**

1. Nadira needs _____.	$25	a learner's permit
2. She makes (a/an) _____.	appointment	test
3. Her appointment is on _____.	Tuesday	Thursday
4. The test is _____.	$26	26¢

C **Complete the learner's permit form about you.**

1. **Name** _____
             LAST   FIRST   MI

2. **Address** _____
             STREET   CITY   STATE   ZIP

3. **Telephone Number** __(_____)_____
                     AREA CODE

4. **Date of birth** _____/_____/_____ 5. ☐ male ☐ female
               MM/DD/YY

6. **Eye color** _____ 7. **Hair color** _____

8. **Glasses?** ☐ yes ☐ no
                          _____
                          SIGNATURE

Road Signs

 A **Listen.**

1.

2.

3.

4.

5.

H = Hospital

6.

Listen and repeat.

B **Circle the problem.**

1.

a.

b.

2.
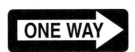

a.

b.

MY LIFE **Copy a sign in your neighborhood.**

Tell your group what it means.

8 How often does the train leave?

Numbers

 A **Listen.**

Carlos: How often does the **B Train** leave?
Clerk: It leaves every **hour**.
Carlos: Oh good. At **4:00, 5:00, and 6:00**.

Grace: How often does the **5 Bus** leave?
Clerk: It leaves every **half hour**.
Grace: Oh good. At **12:00, 12:30, and 1:00**.

Tien: How often does the **subway** leave?
Clerk: It leaves every **15 minutes**.
Tien: Oh good. At **10:15, 10:30, and 10:45**.

Listen and repeat.

B **Match.**

1. ____ 9:00   10:00   11:00   **a.** every 15 minutes

2. ____ 6:45   7:15   7:45   **b.** every half hour

3. ____ 3:30   3:45   4:00   **c.** every hour

C **Talk with 3 classmates.**

A: How often does the _____ leave?
B: It leaves every _____.
A: Oh good. At _____.

Word List

bus to Miami / hour
train to New York / half hour
M-109 bus / 15 minutes

Unit 12

9 A Bus Schedule

 A **Listen and read.**

WEEKDAYS	BUS K-52 LEAVES		INBOUND	
Pond Street	**Westside Park**	**City Library**	**Weston School**	**Midway Airport**
4:30	4:45	5:00	5:15	5:45
4:45	5:00	5:15	5:30	6:00
5:00	5:15	5:30	5:45	6:15
5:15	5:30	5:45	6:00	6:30
5:30	5:45	6:00	6:15	6:45

This is a schedule for the K-52 bus. It leaves Pond Street every 15 minutes. The bus goes to Westside Park, City Library, Weston School, and Midway Airport. It's 4:35. The next bus leaves Pond Street at 4:45.

Read with a partner.

B **Look at the bus schedule in Activity A. Answer the questions.**

1. When does the bus leave Pond Street? _____ 4:30, 4:45, 5:00, 5:15, and 5:30 _____

2. When does the bus leave Weston School? _____

3. It's 4:20. When does the next bus leave Pond Street? _____

4. It's 4:00. When does the next bus leave Westside Park? _____

5. It's 5:10. When does the next bus leave City Library? _____

6. It's 5:20. When does the next bus leave Weston School? _____

7. It's 6:35. When does the next bus leave Midway Airport? _____

8. It's 5:35. When does the next bus leave City Library? _____

Grammar: Questions with *Be*

  A **Listen and read.**

QUESTIONS WITH *Be*		
Questions		**Short Answers**
What is the name of your school?		City College.
Where is the school?		On First Avenue.
When is your class?		At 6:00 P.M.
Who is the teacher?		Sandy Johnson.

Listen and repeat.

  B **Listen and complete.**

Who	What	When	~~Where~~

1. **A:** _____Where_____ is the school?   **B:** Newark.
2. **A:** _____ is your classmate's name?   **B:** Yuri.
3. **A:** _____ is your teacher?   **B:** Jon Friedman.
4. **A:** _____ is the class?   **B:** On Wednesday at 3:00.

Read with a partner.

C **Complete.**

1. **A:** _____What_____ do you study?   **B:** English.
2. **A:** _____ do you study English?   **B:** On Monday at 9:00.
3. **A:** _____ is your school?   **B:** In Los Angeles.
4. **A:** _____ is your teacher?   **B:** _____.

11 Grammar: Questions with *Do/Does*

  A **Listen and read.**

QUESTIONS WITH *Do*	
Questions	**Short Answers**
How do you **get** to Miami?	By train.
What train **do** you **take**?	The M-101.
When do the trains for Miami **leave**?	At 7:05 A.M.
Where do I get the train to Miami?	At Track 3.

QUESTIONS WITH *Does*	
Questions	**Short Answers**
How does Carlos **get** to Miami?	By train.
What time **does** the train **leave**?	At 7:05.
When does the train for Miami **leave**?	At 10:05.
Where does he **get** the train to Miami?	At Track 3.

B **Match.**

> **a.** By bus.   **b.** It arrives at 12:15.   **c.** The K-52.   **d.** It goes to the station.

1. _b_ When does the bus arrive?   2. ____ What bus do you take?

3. ____ How do you get to school?   4. ____ Where does the bus go?

C **Complete.**

1. **A:** _What time_ does the train leave?   **B.** It leaves at 7:45.

2. **A:** _____ does the train from Rio arrive?   **B.** It arrives at 8:00.

3. **A:** _____ do you get to school?   **B.** I get to school by bus.

4. **A:** _____ does the D-105 bus go?   **B.** It goes to Phoenix.

A **Listen and read.**

   Ben and Grace were at the hospital last night. Now they are leaving. They are driving home with their new baby boy. His name is Adam Lee.

   Ben and Grace want Adam to be safe. They put him in a baby car seat. Car seats help babies to be safe in cars. The car seat was a present. It was a present from their friends at school. Their friends want Adam to be safe in cars.

   Adam is safe in his car seat. Ben and Grace are safe in the car, too. They always use their seat belts. Now the family can drive home.

Read with a partner.

B ✔ **Check.**

What's a good title for this story?

_____ **1.** Use Car Seats and Belts   _____ **2.** Fun Presents for Babies

C **Answer the questions.**

1. When were Ben and Grace at the hospital?   _____ Last night _____

2. Where are they going now?   _____

3. What keeps Adam safe in the car?   _____

4. Who gave the car seat to Ben and Grace?   _____

5. How often do Ben and Grace use their seat belts?   _____

A **Listen and read.**

This is Paul's story. It's about getting to school.

Getting to School
by Paul Lemat

In my country, my family lives near school. My sisters and I usually walk to school. My friend Franz lives far from school. He rides a bike.

Now I live far from school. I take a bus and a subway. My bus stop is on 25th Street. I take the G-203 bus to Pine Avenue. Then I take the subway to Baker Street. Then I walk on Baker Street to 29th Avenue. My school is on Baker and 29th.

Some classmates take buses. Some classmates take subways. Leo drives his taxicab to school. Leo sometimes drives Maria in his taxicab.

Read with a partner.

B **Write about you.**

How do students get to school in your native country?
How do you and your classmates get to school now?

_____

_____

_____

_____

_____

How do you get to school? 203

What do you know?

 A **Listen and write.**

A. Excuse me. _____ is the drugstore?

B. It's on the _____. Next to the movie theater.

 B **Listen and fill in the answer sheet.**

1. **A.** ride a bike   **B.** take the subway
2. **A.** school   **B.** the bus stop
3. **A.** the next bus   **B.** next to the drugstore
4. **A.** the Blue Line   **B.** the Blue Train
5. **A.** to the left   **B.** straight ahead
6. **A.** every 15 minutes   **B.** every 50 minutes

ANSWER SHEET

1. Ⓐ ⬤Ⓑ
2. Ⓐ Ⓑ
3. Ⓐ Ⓑ
4. Ⓐ Ⓑ
5. Ⓐ Ⓑ
6. Ⓐ Ⓑ

C **Complete the road signs. Write what they mean.**

1.

Go one way.

2.

_____

3.

_____

4.

_____

D Write 4 questions. Ask a partner.

Questions	Answers
What **time do you eat dinner?** .	7:00 P.M.
Who	
When	
Where	
What	

F ✔ Check what you know.

Learning Log

—— across from	—— learner's permit	—— seat belt
—— airport	—— leave	—— speed limit
—— appointment	—— left	—— stop
—— arrive	—— minute	—— straight ahead
—— behind	—— near	—— subway
—— between	—— next to	—— taxicab
—— bike	—— no parking	—— test
—— bus	—— one way	—— train
—— car seat	—— ride	—— walk
—— drive	—— right	—— what
—— every	—— road sign	—— when
—— half hour	—— safety	—— where
—— hospital	—— schedule	—— who
—— hour		

LOOKING BACK Look at page 190. What do you see? Tell a partner.

Review for Units 10–12

A Write *was* or *were*.

1. Sandy _____was_____ a student in 1978.

2. Leo _____ a taxi driver in Russia.

3. Ben and you _____ construction workers in China.

4. My brother and sister _____ office workers in Vietnam.

5. Mariz and I _____ high school students in Haiti.

6. Maria _____ a cashier in Mexico.

7. I _____ a _____ in 2007.

SIMPLE PAST OF *BE*
Questions
I **was** a student.   He **was** a student.   She **was** a student.
You **were** students.   We **were** students.   They **were** students.

B Write *can* or *can't*.

1. Nadira has a learner's permit. She _____can_____ learn to drive now.

2. Carlos doesn't have a driver's license. He _____ drive a taxicab.

3. Isabel is an office worker. She _____ use a computer.

4. Maria speaks Spanish and English. She _____ speak Chinese.

5. Sandy has a fever. She _____ play basketball today.

6. Grace's hand hurts. She _____ write.

7. Tien is a delivery person. She _____ drive a van.

8. Ben is a construction worker. He _____ fix things.

C Talk in groups.

What are three things you *can* do? What are three things you *can't* do?

D Match.

1. __c__ What's the matter?
2. ____ Can Dr. Green see my son today?
3. ____ What do you do?
4. ____ What was your job before?
5. ____ Can you use a computer?
6. ____ How do you get to school?
7. ____ Where's the bus stop?
8. ____ When does the next bus leave?

a. I was a cashier.
b. I'm a computer programmer.
c. I have a headache.
d. Yes. Dr. Green can see him at 2:00.
e. On Third Street.
f. It leaves at 10:15.
g. Yes, I can.
h. I take the bus.

E Listen. Complete. Write the time.

a backache	a cold	a fever	a headache
an infection	a sore throat	a toothache	

Name	What's the matter?	When is the appointment?
1. Grace	a cold	11:00
2. Paul		
3. Tien		
4. Carlos		
5. Maria		
6. Isabel		
7. Jane		

A Circle the types of transportation. <u>Underline</u> the country.

Scooters in Italy

A subway in Japan

A tuk-tuk in Laos

A taxicab in the USA

Bicycles in China   A bus in India

B Think about it. What transportation do you use to go to the places in the box? Complete the chart.

~~school~~	work	shopping
the doctor	the post office	my friend's house
home		

My native country	the USA
I go to school by bicycle.	

C Talk in groups.

In my native country I go to school by bus. In the US I go to school by car.

209

Listening Script

Note: This listening script contains audio support for many of the activities in Student Book. When the words on the Student Book page are identical to those on the audio program, a listening script is not provided.

Unit 1: Welcome to the Classroom.

Page 4

D. Listen and write.
1. a-b-c
2. d-e-f
3. g-h-i
4. j-k-l
5. m

Page 5

C. Listen and say the letters.
1. USA U-S-A
2. China C-H-I-N-A
3. Haiti H-A-I-T-I
4. Russia R-U-S-S-I-A
5. Brazil B-R-A-Z-I-L
6. Mexico M-E-X-I-C-O
7. Colombia C-O-L-O-M-B-I-A
8. Somalia S-O-M-A-L-I-A
9. Vietnam V-I-E-T-N-A-M

D. Listen and write.
1. h-i
2. y-o-u
3. n-a-m-e
4. f-r-o-m
5. w-r-i-t-e
6. h-e-l-l-o

Page 10

A. Listen.
1. Open. Open the book.
2. Close. Close the book.
3. Take out. Take out the pen.
4. Put away. Put away the book.
5. Go to. Go to the board.

6. Point to. Point to the computer.

Listen and repeat.
1. open
2. close
3. take out
4. put away
5. go to
6. point to

B. Listen and circle.
1. Take out the paper.
2. Put away the book.
3. Open the book.
4. Close the door.

Page 11

A. Listen and fill in.
1. Open the door.
2. Go to the board.
3. Take out the pen.
4. Put away the notebook.
5. Open the door.
6. Put away the paper.
7. Point to the desk.
8. Take out the book.

Page 12

E. Listen and circle.
1. Six
2. Five
3. Ten
4. 5 Pen Avenue
5. 555-5050
6. (781) 555-9876

Page 14

A. Listen and circle.
1. **Sandy:** What's this?
   Isabel: A chair.
2. **Isabel:** What is this?
   Sandy: A desk.

3. **Leo:** Hi, I'm Leo.
4. **Ben:** Hello. I am Ben.
5. **Tien:** My name is Tien. I am from Vietnam.
6. **Paul:** My name is Paul. I'm from Haiti.
7. **Nestor:** It's my homework.
8. **Maria:** It is complete.

Page 16

A. Listen and write.
Sandy: Hello. I'm Sandy. What's your name?
Ben: My name is Ben.
Sandy: Nice to meet you, Ben.
Ben: Nice to meet you too, Sandy.

B. Listen and circle.
1. Go to the board.
2. Close the book.
3. My first name is Leo.
4. I-S-A-B-E-L
5. I live at 2039 Board Street.

C. Listen and complete
Sandy: Hi. I'm Sandy. What's your name?
Grace: My name is Grace Lee.
Sandy: How do you spell that?
Grace: My first name is G-R-A-C-E. My last name is L-E-E.

Page 17

D. Listen and write.
1. Name n-a-m-e
2. Close c-l-o-s-e
3. Board b-o-a-r-d
4. Book b-o-o-k
5. Ten t-e-n
6. Seven s-e-v-e-n

Unit 2: Where are you from?

Page 22

A. Listen.
1. Married. Grace is married.
2. Single. Paul is single.
3. Divorced. Leo is divorced.
4. Widowed. Maria is widowed.

Listen and repeat.
1. married
2. single
3. divorced
4. widowed

B. Listen and circle.
1. They are married.
2. He's widowed.
3. They are single.
4. They are divorced.

Page 23

A. Listen.
Paul: I am average height. Leo is tall. Tien is short.
Tien: Paul and Carlos are average height.

Listen and repeat.
average height
tall
short

Page 25

B. Listen. Write the number.
1. He has brown hair and brown eyes. He's from Brazil.
2. He has gray hair. He's divorced.
3. She is tall. She's Somali.
4. She has red hair. She's from the USA.

Page 32

A. Listen and write.
Grace: I am tall.
Leo: I speak Russian.
Tien: I have glasses.
Isabel: I have blond hair. I have blue eyes.
Sandy: He has brown hair.
Paul: You come from Somalia.
Ben: We have brown eyes.

B. Listen and fill in.
1. I speak Vietnamese.
2. Leo is divorced.
3. Maria speaks Spanish.
4. What is your address?

Unit 3: This is my family.

Page 35

A. Listen.
1. **Sandy:** Father. This is my father.
2. **Sandy:** Mother. This is my mother.
3. **Sandy:** Brother. This is my brother.
4. **John:** Sister. This is my sister.
5. **Sandy:** Daughter. This is my daughter.
6. **Sandy:** Son. This is my son.

Listen and repeat.
1. mother
2. father
3. brother
4. sister
5. daughter
6. son

Page 36

A. Listen.
Sandy's Family Tree
Arthur is Sandy's father.
Ann is Sandy's mother.
Tomiko is John's wife.
John is Tomiko's husband.
Sandy is Will's wife.
Will is Sandy's husband.
Sara is Tomiko and John's daughter.
Miles is Tomiko and John's son.
Andy, Justin, and Jane are Sandy and Will's children.

B. Listen and write.
1. **Sandy:** Arthur is my father.
2. **John:** Ann is my mother.
3. **Will:** Sandy is my wife.
4. **Tomiko:** John is my husband.
5. **Sandy:** Justin is my son.
6. **Will:** Jane is my daughter.
7. **John:** Sara and Miles are my children.

Page 38

A. Listen and read.
Grandfather. This is Carlos's grandfather.
Grandmother. This is Carlos's grandmother.
Uncle. This is Carlos's uncle.
Aunt. This is Carlos's aunt.
Cousin. This is Carlos's cousin.
Parents. These are Carlos's parents.

Listen and repeat.
grandfather
grandmother
uncle
aunt
cousin
parents

B. Listen and circle.
1. My name is Carlos. These are my relatives.
2. This is my grandfather. His name is Umberto.
3. This is my grandmother. Her name is Vera.
4. This is my uncle. His name is Ricardo.
5. This is my aunt. Her name is Celina.
6. This is my cousin. His name is Alfredo.
7. These are my parents. Their names are Magda and Rudolfo.

Page 44

B. Listen and circle.
1. **Sandy:** Do you have a sister?
   Leo: Yes, I do.
2. **Ben:** Do you have two brothers?
   Tien: No, I don't.
3. **Paul:** Do you have a young daughter?
   Sandy: Yes, I do.
4. **Nadira:** Do you have a tall uncle?
   Carlos: Yes, I do.

Page 45

B. Listen and circle.
1. Her name is Ann.
2. His name is Will.
3. Your name is Tomiko.
4. Her name is Jane.

Page 48

A. Listen and fill in.
1. My name is Ms. Tanaka.
2. I live at 60 Brown Road.
3. I am married.
4. My husband's name is John.

5. We have two children.
6. My brother has five children.

B. Listen and fill in.
1. Tien's grandmother is 60 years old.
2. Mr. Avila is Carlos's grandfather.
3. Her name is Ms. Tanaka.
4. Sandy is your teacher.
5. Their names are Paul, Jessie, and Marie.

C. Listen and circle.
1. eighty
2. sixty
3. nineteen
4. twenty-five
5. seventeen
6. twelve
7. fourteen
8. fifty

Review Units 1–3
Page 51

E. Listen and circle.
1. Mary is young. She has red hair. She is single.
2. Peter is old. He has gray hair. He is single.
3. Ellen is young. She has black hair. She is married.
4. Mario is middle-aged. He has brown hair. He is single.

Unit 4: Welcome to our house.
Page 55

A. Listen.
1. Kitchen. It's in the kitchen.
2. Living room. It's in the living room.

3. Bedroom. It's in the bedroom.
4. Dining room. It's in the dining room.
5. Bathroom. It's in the bathroom.
6. Backyard. It's in the backyard.

Listen and repeat.
1. kitchen
2. living room
3. bedroom
4. dining room
5. bathroom
6. backyard

Page 56

A. Listen.
1. Table. Is there a table in the dining room?
2. Sofa. Is there a sofa in the living room?
3. Bed. Is there a bed in the bedroom?
4. Lamp. Is there a lamp in the bedroom?
5. Air conditioner. Is there an air conditioner in the living room?
6. Fireplace. Is there a fireplace in the living room?
7. Dresser. Is there a dresser in the bedroom?
8. Rug. Is there a rug in the bedroom?

Listen and repeat.
1. table
2. sofa
3. bed
4. lamp
5. air conditioner
6. fireplace
7. dresser
8. rug

Page 57

A. Listen.
1. Shower. This is a shower.
2. Sink. This is a sink.
3. Stove. This is a stove.
4. Window. This is a window.
5. Microwave. This is a microwave.
6. Closet. This is a closet.
7. Refrigerator. This is a refrigerator.
8. Tub. This is a tub.

Listen and repeat.
1. shower
2. sink
3. stove
4. window
5. microwave
6. closet
7. refrigerator
8. tub

B. Listen and circle.
1. There's a refrigerator in the kitchen.
2. There's a sink in the kitchen.
3. There's a tub in the bathroom.
4. There's a window in the dining room.
5. There's a closet in the bedroom.
6. There's a microwave in the kitchen.

Page 58

A. Listen.
1. **Paul:** A house. I live in a house.
2. **Isabel:** A rented room. I live in a rented room.
3. **Tien:** An apartment. I live in an apartment.

Listen and repeat.
1. a house
2. a rented room
3. an apartment

Page 60

A. Listen and circle.
1. Where do you eat?
2. Where do you sleep?
3. Where do you shower?
4. Where do you cook?

Page 61

A. Listen.
1. In the city. Leo's dream house is in the city.
2. In the country. Isabel's dream house is in the country.
3. At the beach. Paul's dream house is at the beach.
4. In the suburbs. Nadira's dream house is in the suburbs.

Listen and repeat.
1. in the city
2. in the country
3. at the beach
4. in the suburbs

Page 62

B. Listen and circle.
1. sixty
2. nineteen
3. forty
4. eighteen
5. thirteen
6. seventy
7. twelve
8. fifty

C. Listen and write.
1. My address is 50 Beach Street.

2. The house is 70 years old.
3. The rented room is at 20 Green Street.
4. There are 13 apartments.
5. There are 19 windows.
6. I have 12 tables.
7. We need 40 chairs in the dining room.
8. Ben has 14 pens.
9. The house has 18 rooms.
10. There are 17 lamps in the garage.

Page 63

B. Listen and match.
Sandy's students are at a garage sale. What do they need?
1. Isabel needs a lamp.
2. Carlos needs a backpack.
3. Ben needs some CDs.
4. Grace needs a bike.

Page 64

A. Listen and check.
1. Apartment. I live in an apartment.
2. Rooms. My apartment has two rooms.
3. Kitchen. There is one kitchen.
4. Bedroom. There is one bedroom.
5. Closets. There are four closets.
6. Shower. There is a shower in the bathroom.
7. Families. Five families live in the building.
8. Seventies. My grand-mother is in her seventies.

Page 68

A. Listen and circle.
1. There is a sink in the bathroom.
2. There are books in the bedroom.
3. Paul lives in the city.
4. Nadira is 30.

B. Listen and fill in.
1. Maria is in the dining room.
2. Is there a lamp in the living room?
3. Do you need a rug?
4. Do you need two dressers?

Unit 5: I talk on the phone.

Page 71

B. Listen and circle.
1. **Sandy:** What do you do every day, Leo?
   Leo: I read the newspaper.
2. **Sandy:** What do you do every day, Paul?
   Paul: I brush my teeth.
3. **Sandy:** What do you do every day, Carlos?
   Carlos: I listen to music.
4. **Sandy:** What do you do every day, Maria?
   Maria: I eat breakfast.

Page 72

B. Listen and circle.
1. Ben and Grace study on Monday.
2. Leo cooks dinner on Thursday.
3. Maria and Carlos go to garage sales on Sunday.

4. Nadira and Sandy watch TV on Saturday.

C. Listen and complete.
1. Paul plays soccer on Thursday.
2. Carlos and Ben go to school on Friday.
3. Isabel and Grace go to garage sales on Saturday.
4. Leo and Maria go to class on Monday.
5. Nadira cooks dinner on Tuesday.

Page 74

A. Listen.
1. Ten o'clock. It's ten o'clock.
2. Seven fifteen. It's seven fifteen.
3. One forty-five. It's one forty-five.
4. Three thirty. It's three thirty.
5. Two o'clock. It's two o'clock.
6. Four forty-five. It's four forty-five.
7. Twelve thirty. It's twelve thirty.
8. Eight fifteen. It's eight fifteen.
9. Nine twenty. It's nine twenty.

Listen and repeat.
1. ten o'clock
2. seven fifteen
3. one forty-five
4. three thirty
5. two o'clock
6. four forty-five
7. twelve thirty
8. eight fifteen
9. nine twenty

Page 75

A. Listen.
1. Six o'clock. It's six o'clock.
2. Eight fifteen. It's eight fifteen.
3. Three thirty. It's three thirty.
4. Five forty-five. It's five forty-five.

Listen and repeat.
1. six o'clock
2. eight fifteen
3. three thirty
4. five forty-five

B. Listen and circle.
1. It's six thirty.
2. She eats breakfast at eight thirty.
3. She goes to school at twelve forty-five.
4. They study at two fifteen.
5. Carlos reads the newspaper at four o'clock.
6. He goes to sleep at nine fifteen.

Page 76

C. Listen and write the times.
Grace: I'd like to make an appointment for a haircut.
Man: Can you come on Monday at five thirty?
Grace: Monday at five thirty? That's fine.
Grace: I'd like to make an appointment for a tune-up.
Woman: Can you come on Wednesday at three o'clock?
Grace: Wednesday at three o'clock? That's fine.
Grace: I'd like to make an appointment for a checkup.
Man: Can you come on Friday at one fifteen?
Grace: Friday at one fifteen? That's fine.

Page 78

C. Listen and circle.
1. Paul lives on Fifth Street.
2. Tien lives on Third Avenue.
3. Go to Twelfth Street.
4. The garage sale is on Fourteenth Street.
5. I live on Thirteenth Street.
6. Grace lives on First Avenue.

Page 80

B. Listen and circle.
1. She takes photos.
2. It eats cake.
3. We say "Happy Birthday."
4. I open my presents.
5. Paul calls Isabel on the phone.

Page 84

A. Listen and write.
1. My birthday is October twelfth.
2. Paul's birthday is July fourth.
3. My class is at four thirty.
4. I study on Tuesday.

B. Listen and fill in.
1. Ben is Chinese.
2. Leo reads the newspaper.
3. We talk on the phone.
4. They eat breakfast every day.
5. Jane cooks dinner.
6. It's ten o'clock.
7. Leo's birthday is September third.
8. Nadira has class on Thursday.

C. Listen and circle.
1. Can you come at seven o'clock?
2. He lives on Sixth Street.

3. The house is on Eleventh Street.
4. I go to school at two thirty.
5. My birthday is May thirteenth.
6. I go to school at nine forty-five.
7. He always wakes up at eight o'clock.
8. This is my third English class.
9. Linda's address is 50 G Street.
10. She lives on the 13th floor.

Page 85

E. Listen and write.
Checkup Appointment
On: Monday, April 21 at eight A.M.
Edward J. Weiss, D.D.S.
517 Old Road

Jane's Haircuts
Tuesday to Saturday
nine thirty A.M. to six P.M.
310 Cook Road

Unit 6: Let's go shopping.

Page 87

A. Listen.
1. A shirt. Paul is looking for a shirt.
2. A coat. Tien is looking for a coat.
3. A sweater. Isabel is looking for a sweater.
4. Shoes. Grace is looking for shoes.
5. A watch. Leo is looking for a watch.
6. A dress. Maria is looking for a dress.

7. Pants. Ben is looking for pants.
8. A suit. Carlos is looking for a suit.

Listen and repeat.
1. a shirt
2. a coat
3. a sweater
4. shoes
5. a watch
6. a dress
7. pants
8. a suit

Page 88

A. Listen.
1. A blouse. Isabel needs a blouse.
2. A bathing suit. Carlos needs a bathing suit.
3. A skirt. Grace needs a skirt.
4. A belt. Tien needs a belt.
5. A jacket. Paul needs a jacket.
6. A cap. Leo needs a cap.
7. Socks. Maria needs socks.
8. A scarf. Nadira needs a scarf.

Listen and repeat.
1. a blouse
2. a bathing suit
3. a skirt
4. a belt
5. a jacket
6. a cap
7. socks
8. a scarf

Page 89

B. Listen and circle.
1. Leo has black shoes.
2. Ben has a blue sweater.
3. Maria has a green blouse.
4. Isabel has a purple jacket.

5. Sandy has a pink bathing suit.
6. Tien has a black skirt.

Page 92

A. Listen.
1. Small. The red shirt is small.
2. Medium. The blue shirt is medium.
3. Large. The green shirt is large.

Listen and repeat.
1. small
2. medium
3. large

B. Listen and circle.
1. The pink sweater is large.
2. The black socks are small.
3. The white shirt is small.
4. The red skirt is medium.
5. Grace's yellow blouse is small.
6. Paul's blue pants are large.
7. My purple jacket is medium.
8. Tien's yellow bathing suit is small.

Page 93

A. Listen.
1. Too short. The pants are too short.
2. Too long. The pants are too long.
3. Too small. The jacket is too small.
4. Too big. The shirt is too big.

Listen and repeat.
1. too short
2. too long
3. too small
4. too big

Page 97

A. Listen.
Big sale today only. 50 percent off. A large hat, a brown jacket, black boots, a purple dress, yellow shoes, a green sweater, a blue men's suit, a pink blouse, a red skirt. It's a very big sale!

Page 98

A. Listen and read.
A. Children's pants. Sizes: small, medium, large. Colors: blue, red, or brown. Price: Eighteen dollars and seventy-five cents.
B. Women's sweaters and skirts. Women's sweaters. Sweater sizes: small, medium, large. Sweater colors: green or red. Price: $22. Women's skirts. Skirt sizes: small, medium, large. Skirt colors: brown, green, or blue. Price: $22.95.
C. Men's suits. Sizes: small, medium, large, extra large. Colors: brown, black, or blue. Price: $62.50.

Page 100

A. Listen and match.
1. I have a purple skirt with a white blouse.
2. I have blue pants, a green shirt, and white shoes.
3. I have a brown dress and a long scarf.
4. I have brown pants and a yellow T-shirt.

B. Listen and fill in.
1. I'm a medium.
2. He's wearing shoes.
3. It's a black suit.
4. It's thirty dollars and twenty-five cents.

Unit 7: I'm so hungry!
Page 107

A. Listen.
1. Eggs. We need some eggs.
2. Ice cream. We need some ice cream.
3. Carrots. We need some carrots.
4. Apples. We need some apples.
5. Potatoes. We need some potatoes.
6. Milk. We need some milk.
7. Rice. We need some rice.
8. Beef. We need some beef.
9. Bananas. We need some bananas.

Listen and repeat.
1. eggs
2. ice cream
3. carrots
4. apples
5. potatoes
6. milk
7. rice
8. beef
9. bananas

Page 108

A. Listen.
1. Cake. Do we need some cake?
2. Bread. Do we need some bread?
3. Fish. Do we need some fish?
4. Chicken. Do we need some chicken?
5. Lettuce. Do we need some lettuce?
6. Oranges. Do we need some oranges?
7. Butter. Do we need some butter?

8. Cheese. Do we need some cheese?
9. Pasta. Do we need some pasta?
10. Beans. Do we need some beans?

Listen and repeat.
1. cake
2. bread
3. fish
4. chicken
5. lettuce
6. oranges
7. butter
8. cheese
9. pasta
10. beans

Page 109

B. Listen and complete the chart.
1. Apples are in aisle 1.
2. Beef is in aisle 2.
3. Chicken is in aisle 2.
4. Cheese is in aisle 4.
5. Cake is in aisle 3.
6. Milk is in aisle 4.
7. Lettuce is in aisle 1.

Page 110

A. Listen.
1. Breakfast. At 7:00 I eat breakfast.
2. Lunch. At 12:30 I eat lunch.
3. Dinner. At 6:45 I eat dinner.

Listen and repeat.
1. breakfast
2. lunch
3. dinner

Page 114

A. Listen.
1. A bottle. This is a bottle of oil.
2. A can. This is a can of tomato soup.
3. A bag. This is a bag of rice.
4. A box. This is a box of cereal.
5. A carton. This is a carton of milk.
6. A jar. This is a jar of peanut butter.

Listen and repeat.
1. a bottle
2. a can
3. a bag
4. a box
5. a carton
6. a jar

B. Listen and circle.
1. I need a box of cereal.
2. We need a bag of rice.
3. Do we need a can of soup?
4. They need a carton of milk.
5. She needs a jar of peanut butter.
6. Paul needs a bottle of oil.

Page 116

B. Listen and circle.
1. Grace has an orange.
2. Please get a bag of potatoes.
3. I need six bananas.
4. There are two desserts for lunch today.
5. Paul has two boxes of cereal.
6. Leo always has an apple for breakfast.
7. Do you want some cherry pie?

8. Maria makes three lunches for her children.

Page 120

A. Listen and fill in the answer sheet.
1. I need to buy chicken.
2. I need milk for breakfast.
3. I need apples for lunch.
4. I need oranges, too.
5. I need cheese.

B. Listen and fill in the answer sheet.
1. Let's have hamburgers.
2. Do we need fish?
3. What about you?
4. Excuse me.
5. Anything to drink today?
6. Do we need two boxes of cereal?

Unit 8: How's the weather?

Page 123

A. Listen.
1. Sunny. It's sunny.
2. Snowing. It's snowing.
3. Hot. It's hot.
4. Cold. It's cold.
5. Windy. It's windy.
6. Raining. It's raining.

Listen and repeat.
1. It's sunny.
2. It's snowing.
3. It's hot.
4. It's cold.
5. It's windy.
6. It's raining.

Page 124

A. Listen and circle.
1. It's raining.
2. It's hot.

3. It's cold.
4. It's windy.

Page 125

A. Listen.
1. Winter. It's winter.
2. Spring. It's spring.
3. Summer. It's summer.
4. Fall. It's fall.

Listen and repeat.
1. winter
2. spring
3. summer
4. fall

Page 126

A. Listen.
1. Walking. She's walking.
2. Playing soccer. He's playing soccer.
3. Dancing. They're dancing.
4. Reading. She's reading.
5. Swimming. He's swimming.
6. Listening to music. She's listening to music.
7. Cooking. He's cooking.
8. Watching TV. She's watching TV.

Listen and repeat.
1. walking
2. playing soccer
3. dancing
4. reading
5. swimming
6. listening to music
7. cooking
8. watching TV

Page 127

A. Listen and circle.
1. He's cooking.
2. She's reading.
3. They're dancing.
4. He's swimming.

Page 130

A. Listen and write the numbers.
1. It's very hot. It's 105 degrees Fahrenheit. It's 41 degrees Celsius.
2. It's hot. It's 85 degrees Fahrenheit. It's 29 degrees Celsius.
3. It's warm. It's 70 degrees Fahrenheit. It's 21 degrees Celsius.
4. It's cool. It's 50 degrees Fahrenheit. It's 10 degrees Celsius.
5. It's cold. It's 27 degrees Fahrenheit. It's –3 degrees Celsius.

Page 131

A. Listen and read the weather map.
How is the weather around the nation today? It's a cloudy day in Seattle, and the temperature is 40 degrees Fahrenheit. It's raining in Los Angeles, but the temperature is hot—80 degrees. In Dallas, it's 82 degrees. It's a hot, sunny day. It's raining in Chicago, and the temperature is 25 degrees. In Denver, it's 20 degrees Fahrenheit, and it's snowing. New York is cool and cloudy at 40 degrees. And in Miami it's 75 degrees—sunny and hot!

Page 133

B. Listen and complete.
1. They're studying.
2. She's reading.
3. She's pointing.

Page 136

A. Listen and write.
1. How's the weather?
2. It's cold and windy.
3. My favorite season is spring.
4. I'm playing soccer.
5. What are you doing?
6. They like walking in the snow.

B. Listen and fill in the answer sheet.
1. They're dancing.
2. It's snowing in New York.
3. What do you like doing in the fall?
4. It's a windy day.
5. Carlos is listening to music.
6. How's the weather?

C. Listen and circle.
1. It's 60 degrees Fahrenheit.
2. Seattle is windy.
3. It's 55 degrees Fahrenheit in Miami.
4. Dallas is 40 degrees Fahrenheit.
5. It's cold in New York.
6. Los Angeles is sunny.

Unit 9: Where's the Post Office?

Page 139

A. Listen. Look at page 138.
1. Police station. I'm going to the police station.
2. Bank. I'm going to the bank.
3. Drugstore. I'm going to the drugstore.
4. Hospital. I'm going to the hospital.

5. Fire station. I'm going to the fire station.
6. Gas station. I'm going to the gas station.
7. Library. I'm going to the library.
8. Post office. I'm going to the post office.

Listen and repeat.
1. police station
2. bank
3. drugstore
4. hospital
5. fire station
6. gas station
7. library
8. post office

Page 141

A. Listen.
1. Laundromat. Wash your clothes at the laundromat.
2. Movie theater. I'm going to the movie theater.
3. Supermarket. I buy food at the supermarket.
4. Bus stop. Wait for the bus at the bus stop.
5. Park. My children play in the park.
6. Restaurant. Sometimes I eat at a restaurant.

Listen and repeat.
1. laundromat.
2. movie theater.
3. supermarket.
4. bus stop.
5. park.
6. restaurant.

Page 143

C. Listen and write.
1. The bus stop is next to the supermarket.
2. The park is next to the post office.

3. The drugstore is across from the laundromat.
4. The post office is across from the bus stop.
5. The supermarket is between the drugstore and the bus stop.

Page 144

A. Listen.
1. Near. He's near the bus stop.
2. Far from. They're far from the bus stop.

Listen and repeat.
1. near
2. far from

B. Listen and circle.
1. Leo lives near a bank.
2. Carlos lives near a bus stop.
3. Sandy lives far from the city.
4. Paul lives near a fire station.
5. We live far from a movie theater.
6. Tien lives near a post office.

Page 145

A. Listen.
1. See a movie. Where do you see a movie?
2. Buy stamps. Where do you buy stamps?
3. Wash clothes. Where do you wash clothes?
4. Cash a check. Where do you cash a check?

Listen and repeat.
1. see a movie
2. buy stamps
3. wash clothes
4. cash a check

Page 148

B. Listen and check.
1. Isabel lives on Ocean Road.
2. Ocean Road is between 10th and 11th Streets.
3. Leo lives in Hill City.
4. His house is on Bay Street.
5. It is next to a school.
6. It is across from a park, too.

Page 152

A. Listen and write.
1. **Sandy:** Do you live far from a bus stop?
   Tien: No, I don't.
   Sandy: Do you live near a park?
   Tien: Yes, I do.
2. **Isabel:** Excuse me. Where is the police station?
   Leo: It's on 54th Street, across from the park.
   Isabel: Thanks.

B. Listen and fill in the answer sheet.
1. I'm going to the hospital.
2. Where's the fire station?
3. The library is across from the post office.
4. Is there a movie theater in your neighborhood?
5. Where do you wash clothes?
6. Grace is making a deposit.

C. Listen and fill in the answer sheet.
1. **Waiter:** Can I help you?
   Sandy: Yes. A hamburger, please.
2. **Leo:** This is a good movie.
   Paul: Yes, it is.

3. **Teller:** May I help you?
   Grace: I want to make a deposit.
4. **Clerk:** Good morning.
   Ben: Good morning. I want to buy some stamps.
5. **Grace:** I have eight quarters.
   Ben: Good. We can wash the clothes.
6. **Carlos:** Excuse me, I'm looking for bread.
   Clerk: Bread is in aisle 12.

Review Units 7-9

Page 155

D. Listen and circle.
1. **Mother:** Hello?
   Maria: Hi Mother. It's Maria. How are you?
   Mother: I'm fine. How's the weather in Los Angeles?
   Maria: It's raining.
2. **Grace:** Hi, Isabel.
   Isabel: Hi, Grace.
   Grace: What are Carlos and Tien doing?
   Isabel: They're playing soccer.
3. **Ben:** Hello?
   Leo: Hi Ben. It's Leo.
   Ben: Hi, Leo. How's the weather in Chicago?
   Leo: It's cloudy today.
4. **Paul:** Hi, Tien. It's Paul.
   Tien: Hi, Paul.
   Paul: Do you know where Nadira is?
   Tien: She's swimming at the beach.

Unit 10: You need to see a doctor.

Page 159

A. Listen.
1. An earache.
   Ana: I have an earache.
2. A sore throat.
   Will: I have a sore throat.
3. A headache.
   Maria: I have a headache.
4. A broken arm.
   Paul: I have a broken arm.
5. A toothache.
   Carlos: I have a toothache.
6. A stomachache.
   Nadira: I have a stomachache.
7. A backache.
   Ben: I have a backache.
8. A cold.
   Isabel: I have a cold.

Listen and repeat.
1. an earache
2. a sore throat
3. a headache
4. a broken arm
5. a toothache
6. a stomachache
7. a backache
8. a cold

Page 162

C. Listen and check.
1. **Isabel:** Ow! I have a cut on my hand.
   Dr. Brown: Oh, no. You need a bandage.
2. **Carlos:** I have a fever.
   Dr. Brown: Oh, no. You need aspirin.
3. **Don:** Ow! My foot hurts. I have an infection.
   Dr. Brown: Oh, no. You need an antibiotic.
4. **Leo:** Oh, my head is hot. I feel bad. I have a fever.
   Dr. Brown: Oh, no. You need aspirin.
5. **Nadira:** I have a cough.
   Dr. Brown: Oh, no. You need cough syrup.

Page 163

C. Listen. Complete the chart.
1. **Grace:** What's the matter, Leo?
   Leo: I have a cough and a sore throat.
   Grace: That's too bad. You need some cough syrup.
2. **Carlos:** What's the matter, Isabel?
   Isabel: I have a head-ache. My head hurts.
   Carlos: That's too bad. You need aspirin.
3. **Isabel:** What's the matter, Carlos?
   Carlos: I hurt my hand.
   Isabel: That's too bad. You need to see a doctor.
4. **Grace:** What's the matter, Nadira?
   Nadira: I have a cut finger.
   Grace: That's too bad. You need a bandage.

Page 164

A. Listen.
1. Exercise. I exercise.
2. Drink water. I drink water.
3. Don't smoke. I don't smoke.
4. Get enough sleep. I get enough sleep.
5. Eat healthy food. I eat healthy food.
6. Don't eat junk food. I don't eat junk food.

Listen and repeat.
1. Exercise.
2. Drink water.
3. Don't smoke.
4. Get enough sleep.
5. Eat healthy food.
6. Don't eat junk food.

Page 172

B. Listen and fill in the answer sheet.
1. **A:** What's the matter?
   B: I have a headache.
2. **A:** Can Dr. Wall see me today?
   B: Yes. Dr. Wall can see you at 3:00.
3. **A:** I have a stomachache.
   B: Drink hot water.
4. **A:** What's the matter with Sandy?
   B: Her ear hurts.
5. **A:** Are you healthy?
   B: Yes, I exercise and walk every day.

Unit 11: What's your job?

Page 175

A. Listen. Look at Page 174.
1. A sales clerk. He's a sales clerk.
2. A taxi driver. Leo is a taxi driver.
3. A health aide. Nadira's a health aide.
4. A waiter. He's a waiter.
5. A cook. He's a cook.
6. A cashier. She's a cashier.
7. A construction worker. Ben's a construction worker.
8. A delivery person. Tien's a delivery person.
9. An office worker. Isabel's an office worker.
10. A computer programmer. Paul's a computer programmer

Listen and repeat.
1. a sales clerk
2. a taxi driver
3. a health aide
4. a waiter
5. a cook
6. a cashier
7. a construction worker
8. a delivery person
9. an office worker
10. a computer programmer

Page 176

A. Listen.
1. A taxicab. A taxi driver drives a taxicab.
2. An order pad. A waiter writes an order on an order pad.
3. Pots and pans. A cook uses pots and pans.
4. A computer. An office worker types on a computer.
5. A cash register. A cashier uses a cash register.
6. Tools. A construction worker works with tools.

Listen and repeat.
1. a taxicab
2. an order pad
3. pots and pans
4. a computer
5. a cash register
6. tools

C. Listen and circle.
1. **Woman:** I am an office worker. I use a computer.
2. **Man:** I am a construction worker. I use tools.
3. **Man:** I am a taxi driver. I drive a taxicab.
4. **Woman:** I am a cashier. I use a cash register.
5. **Woman:** I am a cook. I use pots and pans.
6. **Man:** I am a waiter. I use an order pad.

Page 177

A. Listen.
1. Indoors. Do you like to work indoors?
2. Outdoors. Do you like to work outdoors?
3. With people. Do you like to work with people?
4. With machines. Do you like to work with machines?

Listen and repeat.
1. indoors
2. outdoors
3. with people
4. with machines

Page 178

A. Listen.
1. Drive. I can drive a car.
2. Fix. I can fix things.
3. Sell. I can sell things.
4. Cook. I can cook food.
5. Use. I can use a computer.
6. Deliver. I can deliver packages.

Listen and repeat.
1. drive
2. fix
3. sell
4. cook
5. use
6. deliver

C. Listen and check the ad from Activity A.
1. Hi, I'm Lina. I'm interested in a cashier job.
2. Hi, I'm Carlos Avila. I like to work with people. I can be a waiter.
3. Hello, Mr. Howard. My name is Pavel Asimov. I work as a cashier at my school cafeteria.
4. Good afternoon, Mrs. Flores. My name is Nadira Shaheed. I am a health care aide. Is the job still open?
5. Hello. My name is Betty Wong. I saw your sign. Do you still need a waiter?
6. Hello. I'm Pablo Ruiz. I can work evenings as your health care aide.

Page 184

B. Listen and circle.
1. Sandy is a teacher.
2. Maria was a health aide a long time ago.
3. Last year Paul was a student in Haiti.
4. Leo was a taxi driver in Russia.
5. He is a taxi driver now, too.
6. Isabel is an office worker.

Page 188

B. Listen and fill in the answer sheet.
1. I'm a construction worker.
2. A waiter writes on an order pad.
3. What did you do before?
4. I was a health aide.

5. **A:** Can you cook a meal?
   B: No, I can't.

Unit 12: How do you get to school?

Page 191

A. Listen.
1. Take a bus. I take a bus to school.
2. Take a subway. I take a subway to school.
3. Ride a bike. I ride a bike to school.
4. Drive a car. I drive a car to school.
5. Walk. I walk to school.
6. Take a taxi. I take a taxi to school.

Listen and repeat.
1. take a bus
2. take a subway
3. ride a bike
4. drive a car
5. walk
6. take a taxi

Page 192

A. Listen.
1. On the left. The movie theater is on the left.
2. Straight ahead. The post office is straight ahead.
3. On the right. The bank is on the right.

Listen and repeat.
1. on the left
2. straight ahead
3. on the right

D. Listen and circle.
1. The bank is on the right.
2. The post office is straight ahead.
3. The movie theater is on the left.

4. The drugstore is on the right.

Page 193

A. Listen.
1. On the corner of. The bank is on the corner of 22nd Street and Pond Street.
2. Next to. The laundromat is next to the bank.
3. Between. The market is between the bank and the post office.
4. Behind. The parking lot is behind the post office.
5. Across from. The bakery is across from the market.
6. Near. The green truck is near 22nd street.

Listen and repeat.
1. on the corner of
2. next to
3. between
4. behind
5. across from
6. near

Page 195

C. Listen and circle.
1. **Man:** When does the next train to Chicago leave?
   Clerk: It leaves at six fourteen.
   Man: At six fourteen? Thanks.
2. **Man:** When does the next train to Los Angeles leave?
   Clerk: It leaves at ten o'clock.
   Man: At ten o'clock? Thanks.
3. **Woman:** When does the next train to Tempe leave?
   Clerk: It leaves at twelve o'clock.

Woman: At twelve o'clock? Thanks.

4. **Woman:** When does the next train to Newark leave?
   Clerk: It leaves at 10:02.
   Woman: At 10:02? Thanks.

5. **Man:** When does the next train to Boston leave?
   Clerk: It leaves at 8:30.
   Man: At 8:30? Thanks.

6. **Woman:** When does the next train to Miami leave?
   Clerk: It leaves at 5:15.
   Woman: At 5:15? Thanks.

7. **Woman:** When does the next train to San Antonio leave?
   Clerk: It leaves at 2:30.
   Woman: At 2:30? Thanks.

8. **Woman:** When does the next train to San Diego leave?
   Clerk: It leaves at 11:03.
   Woman: At 11:03? Thanks.

Page 200

B. Listen and complete.

1. **A:** Where is the school?
   B: Newark.
2. **A:** What is your class-mate's name?
   B: Yuri.
3. **A:** Who is your teacher?
   B: John Freedman.
4. **A:** When is the class?
   B: On Wednesday at 3:00.

Page 204

A. Listen and write.

A: Excuse me. Where is the drugstore?
B: It's on the left. Next to the movie theater.

B. Listen and fill in the answer sheet.

1. I take the subway to work.
2. How do you get to school?
3. When does the next bus to Portland leave?
4. Excuse me. Where is the Blue Line?
5. Central Park is straight ahead.
6. **A:** How often does the train leave?
   B: It leaves every 15 minutes.

Review for Units 10-12

Page 207

E. Listen. Complete. Write the time.

1. **Grace:** Hello. This is Grace Lee. I have a cold. Can Dr. Brown see me today?
   Man: Dr. Brown can see you at 11:00.
   Grace: At 11:00? That's fine. Thank you.
2. **Paul:** This is Paul Lemat. I have a headache. Can the doctor see me today?
   Woman: Yes. Dr. Black can see you at 3:30 this afternoon.
   Paul: At 3:30? Thank you.
3. **Tien:** Hello. This is Tien Lam. I have a toothache. Can I see Dr. Green today?
   Man: Dr. Green can see you at 12:30.
   Tien: At 12:30? Fine.

4. **Carlos:** This is Carlos Avila. I have an infection. Can I see Dr. Brown today?
   Woman: Can you come at 4:15?
   Carlos: 4:15? Yes, I can be there at 4:15.
5. **Maria:** Hello. This is Maria Cruz. I have a backache. Can I see Dr. Brown today?
   Man: Dr. Brown can see you at 1:45.
   Maria: At 1:45? That's fine. Thank you.
6. **Isabel:** This is Isabel Lopez. I need to see the doctor. I have a sore throat.
   Man: Dr. White can see you at 5:15.
   Isabel: At 5:15? I'll be there. Thanks.
7. **Sandy:** This is Sandy Johnson. My daughter Jane has a fever. Can Dr. Red see her today?
   Man: I'm sorry to hear that. Dr. Red can see Jane at 9:45.
   Sandy: At 9:45? That's great. Thank you.

Vocabulary List

Unit 1

address
alphabet
backpack
board
book
chair
check
circle
classroom
close
complete
computer
desk
door
eight
email address
fill in
first
five
four
go to
homework
I'm (I am)
It's (It is)
last
match
meet
name
nice
nine
notebook
numbers
one
open
paper
pen
phone number
point to
put away
read
seven
six
spell
student
take out
teacher
ten
three
two
What's (What is)
write
zero

Unit 2

address
am
are
average height
black
blond
blue
Brazil
brown
China
Chinese
Colombia
country
divorced
eighteen
eleven
eyes
fifteen
fourteen
from
glasses
gray
green
hair
has
have
identification form
is
language
married
Mexico
middle initial
nineteen
Portuguese
red
Russia
seventeen
short
single
sixteen
Somali
Somalia
Spanish
speak
tall
thirteen
twelve
the United States
Vietnam
white
Vietnamese

widowed
zip code

Unit 3

aunt
brother
children
cousin
daughter
do
don't
eighty
family
father
fifty
forty
granddaughter
grandfather
grandmother
have
her
his
husband
middle-aged
Miss
mother
Mr.
Mrs.
Ms.
my
ninety
old
one hundred
relative
seventy
sister
sixty
son
their
thirty
twenty
twenty-eight
twenty-five
twenty-four
twenty-nine
twenty-one
twenty-seven
twenty-six
twenty-three
twenty-two
uncle
wife

young
your

Our Cultures (Units 1–3)

bow
hug
kiss
say hello
shake hands
wave

Unit 4

air conditioner
apartment
backyard
balcony
bathroom
beach
bed
bedroom
bike
building
city
closet
cook
dining room
dream house
dresser
eat
fan
fireplace
floor
furniture
garage
garage sale
house
kitchen
lamp
living room
microwave
need
pan
refrigerator
rented room
rug
sale
shower
sink
sleep
small

sofa
stove
study
suburbs
table
toaster
tub
window

Unit 5

appointment
April
August
birthday
breakfast
brush
call
checkup
cleaning
clock
comb
date of birth
December
dinner
eat
eighth
eleventh
every day
February
fifth
first
fourteenth
fourth
Friday
give
haircut
home
January
July
June
listen
lunch
March
May
medical history
Monday
movie
newspaper
ninth
November
o'clock
October
often

once a month
once a week
party
people
phone
play
presents
read
Saturday
say
second
September
seventh
shop
sixth
start
study
Sunday
talk
teeth
tenth
third
thirteenth
Thursday
time
Tuesday
tune-up
TV
twelfth
watch
Wednesday
week
work

Unit 6

bathing suit
belt
big
black
blouse
blue
brown
cap
catalog
cent
check
clothes
clothing
coat
color
dime
dollar

dress
favorite
green
help
jacket
large
long
medium
money
nickel
orange
pants
penny
pink
price
purple
quarter
red
scarf
shirt
shoes
shopping list
short
size
skirt
small
socks
suit
sweater
watch
wear
white
yellow

Our Cultures (Units 4–6)

adobe house
apartment building
pole house
Victorian house
house
yurt

Unit 7

aisle
always
apple
apple juice
bag
bakery

banana
beans
beef
bottle
box
bread
breakfast
butter
cake
can
carrot
carton
cereal
cheese
chicken
coffee
container
cost
coupon
dairy
dessert
dinner
egg
fish
fruit
hamburger
hungry
ice cream
jar
lettuce
lunch
meal
meat
milk
oil
orange
pasta
peanut butter
pie
pizza
potato
potluck
produce
rice
sandwich
soda
sometimes
supermarket
sugar
sushi
taco
tea

tomato
tuna
usually
vegetable

Unit 8

Celsius
cloudy
cold
cook
cool
dance
degrees
drink
dry
Fahrenheit
fall
hot
listen
map
music
play
raining
read
season
snowing
soccer
spring
summer
sunny
swim
temperature
walk
warm
watch
weather
weather map
windy
winter

Unit 9

account number
across from
application
ATM (automated
   teller machine)
bank
between
bus stop
buy stamps
cash a check
checking account

corner
deposit
deposit slip
drugstore
excuse me
far from
fire station
gas station
hospital
in
laundromat
library
make a deposit
movie theater
near
neighborhood
next to
on
park
paycheck
PIN (personal
   identification
   number)
police station
post office
restaurant
savings account
see a movie
supermarket
wash clothes
withdrawal

Our Cultures (Units 7–9)

farm stand
fish market
floating market
night market
street market
supermarket

Unit 10

antibiotic
arm
aspirin
backache
bandage
broken arm
capsule
chest
cold

co-payment
cough
cough syrup
cut
drink
drops
ear
earache
enough
exercise
eye
fever
finger
foot
hand
head
headache
health insurance
healthy
home remedy
hurt
infection
insurance card
junk food
leg
lift weights
medicine
nose
once
orange juice
pill
raise
rest
run
sick
sleep
smoke
sore throat
stomach
stomachache
stretch
swim
teaspoon
three times
toes
toothache
touch
twice
water

Unit 11

ago
application
cash register
cashier
caution
computer
computer
  programmer
construction
  worker
cook
deductions
deliver
delivery person
drive
emergency
employer
exit
fire extinguisher
fix
gross pay
health aide
high voltage
indoors
job
job application
keep out
leave
machines
office worker
order pad
outdoors
paycheck
pots and pans
safety signs
sales clerk
sell
soap
take-home pay
taxes
taxicab
taxi driver
tools
use
waiter
want ad
wash hands
work area
yesterday

Unit 12

across from
airport
appointment
arrive
behind
between
bike
bus
car
car seat
drive
every
half hour
hospital
hour
learner's permit
leave
left
minute
near
next to
no parking
one way
ride
right
safety
schedule
seat belt
speed limit
stop
straight ahead
subway
taxicab
test
train
walk
what
when
where
who

Our Cultures (Units 10–12)

bicycle
bus
scooter
subway
taxicab
tuk-tuk

Index

76, 81, 82, 85, 87, 88, 89, 90, 91, 96, 98, 100, 101, 109, 113, 115, 118, 121, 134, 135, 137, 150, 153, 160, 161, 170, 173, 175, 179, 181, 182, 183, 187, 189, 196, 199, 200, 202, 203, 205

Learning Logs: 17, 33, 49, 69, 85, 101, 120, 137, 153, 173, 189, 205

Supporting Skills

Alphabet: 4, 5, 6, 13

Bubbles: 9, 11, 32, 37, 48, 68, 84, 100, 120, 136, 152, 172, 188, 204

Charts: 13, 20, 44, 49, 53, 57, 68, 105, 109, 111, 117, 120, 128, 129, 131, 137, 144, 148, 157, 162, 163, 166, 170, 177, 180, 181, 185, 191, 207, 209

Check: 8, 17, 33, 46, 49, 60, 64, 66, 69, 85, 101, 103, 109, 115, 117, 120, 137, 148, 150, 153, 162, 164, 173, 177, 180, 189, 202, 205

Circle: 8, 10, 12, 14, 16, 22, 30, 38, 44, 45, 46, 48, 51, 57, 60, 62, 65, 68, 71, 72, 75, 78, 80, 82, 84, 89, 92, 102, 112, 114, 116, 124, 127, 136, 144, 147, 155, 166, 176, 180, 182, 184, 192, 195, 196, 197

Conversations: 2, 6, 7, 9, 18, 19, 20, 21, 35, 37, 41, 42, 54, 55, 56, 58, 59, 63, 70, 71, 72, 73, 74, 76, 78, 84, 86, 87, 88, 89, 90, 91, 92, 100, 106, 107, 108, 109, 110, 111, 112, 113, 120, 122, 123, 125, 126, 127, 128, 137, 138, 139, 140, 141, 142, 143, 144, 145, 158, 159, 160, 161, 163, 164, 165, 172, 174, 175, 177, 178, 179, 181, 185, 190, 191, 192, 193, 194, 195, 198

Forms:
    application, 151 (card club), 186 (job)
    census, 43
    emergency, 15
    family, 43
    health, 167
    identification, 27
    medical history, 79

Matching: 4, 9, 51, 63, 93, 97, 103, 176, 180, 183, 194, 201, 207

Sentences: 3, 9, 11, 12, 14, 16, 23, 24, 26, 28, 29, 30, 31, 32, 33, 36, 39, 41, 45, 47, 49, 50, 51, 61, 62, 67, 69, 72, 75, 77, 81, 83, 84, 85, 88, 90, 96, 100, 101, 102, 111, 113, 115, 118, 120, 124, 129, 131, 132, 133, 134, 135, 136, 142, 145, 146, 149, 150, 152, 153, 154, 155, 161, 165, 168, 169, 171, 173, 175, 179, 182,

184, 185, 186, 187, 188, 200, 203, 204, 205, 206

Spelling: 5, 6, 17

Writing the number: 100, 169

Topics

CLASSROOM
Directions, 8, 9, 10, 11
Items, 7, 8, 9
Emergency form, 15

CLOTHING
Colors, 89, 91
Fitting, 93
Types, 87, 88, 90
Sizes, 92

COMMUNITY RESOURCES
Fire station, 139, 140
Health services, 139, 140
Library, 139, 140
Police department, 139, 140
Post office, 139, 140
Public transportation, 141, 191, 194

CULTURES
Our Cultures, 53-53, 104-105, 156-157, 208-209

EMPLOYMENT
Application forms, 186
Interviews, 179, 187
Past experience, 181
Paychecks, 182
Professions, 175
Safety signs, 183
Skills, 178
Tools and equipment, 176
Want ads, 180
Work environment, 177

FOOD
Containers, 114
Food groups, 109
Groceries, 107, 108
Meals and mealtimes, 110, 11, 113
Ordering a meal, 112
Potlucks, 115
Restaurants, 112
Types, 107, 108, 112

Photo Credits for Taking Off Student Book, 2nd edition